W9-BMY-637

THE

BOHO

MANIFESTO

BS

MA

THE BOHO MANIFESTO

AN INSIDER'S GUIDE TO
POSTCONVENTIONAL LIVING

JULIA CHAPLIN

ARTISAN | NEW YORK

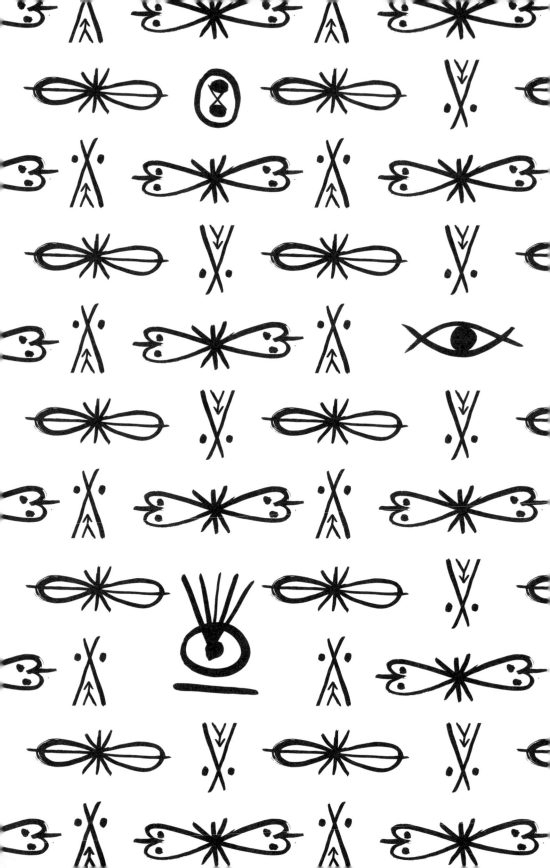

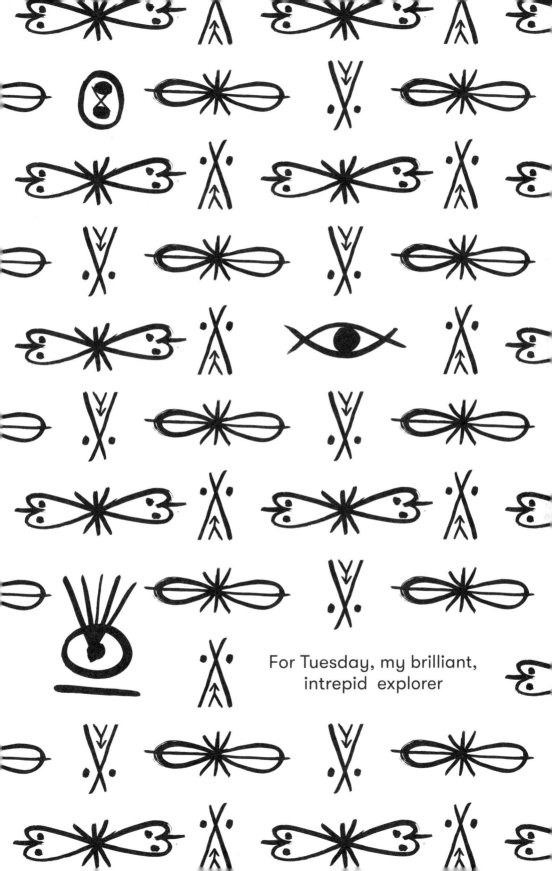

For Tuesday, my brilliant, intrepid explorer

CONTENTS

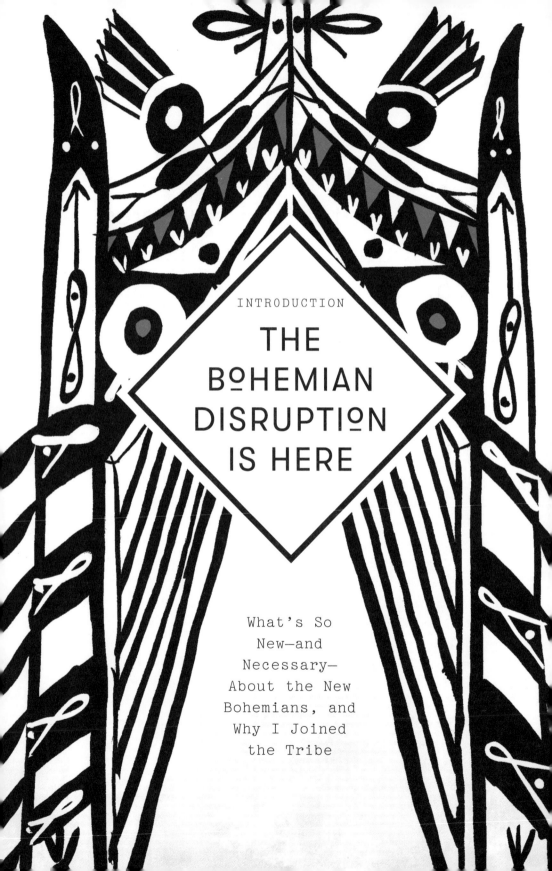

THE BOHEMIAN DISRUPTION IS HERE

What's So New—and Necessary—About the New Bohemians, and Why I Joined the Tribe

We had a white VW van with a motor that sputtered so loud you could hear it coming from blocks away.

My parents were hippies, and we often lived commune-style in big run-down houses, each family staking out a section of rooms. We moved every couple of years: to Cambridge, Massachusetts; Washington, D.C.; Key West, Florida; the Bahamas; and Mexico. When I was caught breaking rules in high school, instead of getting in trouble like normal kids, I was dragged to my mother's astrology circle. "We can understand why you snuck out and lied about going to the concert," they'd say sympathetically, looking over my birth chart. "Mercury was in retrograde." My mom was newly into health food; she would spend hours making tofu in the kitchen one day, but the rest of the week we'd eat Wendy's cheeseburgers and take-out from Pizza Hut. In retrospect, my parents were just experimenting with the new age

philosophies of their time. They'd rejected their own conventional upbringings in claustrophobic, preppy Northeast society but hadn't figured out what to replace it with for my sister and me. So it came out half-baked. And naturally I wanted nothing to do with any of it.

I did love the freedom of it all. Compared to most of my friends, I had hardly any restrictions. And so as an adult, I moved to Manhattan and sought out the glamorous, fast-paced world of fashion, writing for the *New York Times*, *Elle*, *Vogue*, and other publications. But at some point, all the reckless parties and heavily promoted products seemed a bit pointless—mostly—and I began to search for something more. I took up yoga, started attending Burning Man, and learned to surf. I traveled around the world seeking remote, bohemian enclaves where counterculture types were rejecting conventionality and living life on their own terms—sort of like my parents, only better because now it was *my* experiment. I wrote a book series about it called Gypset, a word I made up that means gypsy + jet set, an attempt to fuse my hippie upbringing with my adult life and create something uniquely me. A full-fledged identity search.

I was changing, but so was the world around me. Now freelancers with laptops (my life for over a decade) were called entrepreneurs. Shamans became as common as therapists. Marijuana was referred to as cannabis and began to be legalized. People were questioning materialism and crafting a new aspiration of spirituality and healing of the ecosphere.

In other words, the world was becoming more bohemian. Which is why I decided to write this book, *The Boho Manifesto*: my attempt to pull all of these seemingly disparate elements—neuroscience, tantra, permaculture, barter economy—together and try to find my place in it. It was the neo–Age of Aquarius I had been both waiting for and avoiding—there were so many commonalities with my upbringing. Is AcroYoga cool or silly? What even *is* AcroYoga? There was only one way to find out.

And so I began my immersion. I microdosed. I joined a weekend farming community in upstate New York and planted oats barefoot in the dirt in accordance with the lunar calendar. I attended an ideas festival and learned about Mars colonization and AgTech (agriculture technology). I spent seven days in silence at a Buddhist meditation retreat. I read self-help books and pored over TED Talks on YouTube. I learned the difference between entheogens and adaptogens. I even came up with a few of my own ideas—like microgurus (the concept is that now everyone can be a small-scale guru). But the more I did, the further I got from being done. The new bohemian landscape just kept growing. Of course, this made me happy as it only confirmed that I was on the right track. But it didn't answer my question about whether I thought it was all ridiculous or profound. Because the answer is that it's both. Which is why the contemporary bohemian movement is both compelling and perplexing.

But what does "bohemian" even mean? By definition, bohemians are unconventional people, people who question rules and practices and attempt to come up with something new and better. Or at least test the limits. The word originated in Paris in the 1800s when it was believed incorrectly that Romani people reached France via Bohemia, the western part of the Czech Republic. In Paris, many of the Romani lived in poor, marginal neighborhoods; when a new group of starving artists took up residency alongside them, they were referred to as Bohemians. Henry Murger documented this in *Scènes de la Vie de Bohème*, published as a collection of short stories in 1845. "They are a race of obstinate dreamers for whom art has remained a faith and not a profession," Murger wrote of his bohemians.

Other bohemian time periods included the 1920s in Paris and the 1950s, when Beatnik writers Paul Bowles, Allen Ginsberg, and Jack Kerouac hung out in Greenwich Village, North Beach, and Tangier. The hippie era of the 1960s and '70s was the last great bohemian epoch, the one that most directly inspired this book. The hippies sought to overthrow a hypocritical and outdated society by supporting civil rights, women's rights, gay rights, and protests against the Vietnam War—driven by a search for new and more authentic forms of spirituality, often from Eastern traditions. And much like my parents, the hippies were good at protest and rejection but less adept at coming up with solutions.

The world found in the pages of *The Boho Manifesto* began in the wake of the global economic crash in 2008 that corresponded with the rise of social media, smartphones, and a start-up mentality. The traditional corporate structure began to fade, and in its place, a new DIY mind-set emerged. Meanwhile, the planetary and social problems that the hippies began to address hadn't gone away; they'd only escalated. But this time around, a new generation—organized, wired, and seeking consciousness—is attempting to tackle them. Revolutionaries are now simply called disruptors.

The biggest difference between now and the 1960s is that bohemians aren't fringe anymore. People work within the system, they don't drop out of it, and if they do, they are likely doing it on social media with a couple million followers. What used to be a guru might now be called an "influencer." Unlike Murger's bohemians in Paris, this group likes money. In fact, bohemianism is big business. In his 2000 book, *Bobos in Paradise*, David Brooks argued that bohemianism collided with the mainstream in the 1980s when the Baby Boomer generation of my parents started companies like Microsoft and Patagonia. But things have progressed since then. It's not just about colliding with the mainstream; bohemianism *is* the mainstream—at least the liberal one. What happens when more and more CEOs of Fortune 500 companies microdose or meditate? To be able to effect change from both the inside and out is powerful. Whatever the outcome, this new bohemian era owns a unique place in history—the moment when everything changed. Enjoy!

CHAPTER 1

FREE YOUR MIND

Ayahuasca,
Neuroscience,
and the Art of
Non-Doing

We are feeling a collective pull to heal the earth, heal others, and most important, heal ourselves.

There's no question that something has gone wrong with human civilization. The ice caps are melting, our landfills are full, and the world seems to be becoming ever more toxic, and meanwhile we're all bent over our phones, watching other people's lives, thirsty for "likes." Spirituality is where healing starts. We need something beyond ourselves, something bigger, a higher meaning.

We're witnessing the dawn of a choose-your-own spiritual adventure personalized for our needs, tailored to our experiences, and modified as needed. Maybe you picked up some Buddhism at a workshop at the Esalen Institute (a retreat center in Big Sur), or a bit of Kabbalah at an Israeli camp at Burning Man, or a belief in sorcery at the Damanhur community in the hills of Italy. The point is not to adhere to some orthodox set of teachings but to search for your path of connectedness—the new bohemians are different from hipsters or yuppies or one of those media-invented clichés of the past because they're defined not by consumption but by spirituality. Or at least that's the aspiration.

It means being open to shamans, who figure prominently as liaisons between the plant and human worlds. Plants overlooked for too long are finally having their moment—especially psychedelic ones, from iboga to San Pedro. People are ingesting these ancient ritualistic staples to help them heal and connect.

Meditation works too. But new bohemians are not space cadets: their spiritual journey is backed up by data. Science is legitimizing the benefits of counterculture touchstones such as LSD, yoga, and meditation. Think of it as the Information Age of Aquarius.

MEDITATION:
THE NEW NICE

Group meditation at a Big Quiet event,
North Brooklyn Farms, New York

When I meditate, I'm less likely to fly into a rage, whether over weighty family arguments or daily minutia like letting strangers cut in line. And in that way, meditation actually makes the world a better place, one no longer quite so selfish and panicky.

My pal Dan Harris, an ABC news correspondent who wrote a bestselling book about learning to meditate called *10% Happier: How I Tamed the Voice in My Head, Reduced Stress Without Losing My Edge, and Found Self-Help That Actually Works—A True Story*, explained it to me this way: "Meditation is an exorable process. If you try holding the door open for someone and it feels good, then you're likely to do it again so you can keep feeling good. And that just gets scaled up." So it's not your imagination. More and more people are meditating, and it's having the effect of making the world a "nicer" place.

Science has taken the weird out of meditation and made it a viable way to cut down on dark days and addictive meds.

Research now shows that the old bohemians got something right after all: meditators sleep better, have boosted immune systems, and are less anxious and less depressed than nonmeditators. The UC Davis Center for Mind and Brain, in a recent report, found that meditation affects the brain on a cellular level and is linked to higher levels of telomerase, an enzyme crucial for the long-term health of cells in the body. In a 2011 Harvard-affiliated study using MRIs, researchers discovered that participants who practiced an average of twenty-seven minutes of mindfulness exercises a day over eight weeks had "increased gray-matter density in the hippocampus, known to be important for learning and memory, and in structures associated with self-awareness, compassion, and introspection." And the report noted also "decreased gray-matter density in the amygdala, which is known to play an important role in anxiety and stress." So the answer to "Does it work?" is yes.

I'm not talking about tight superficial smiles—this is deep sincerity. And the good news is, it seems to be contagious.

THE ART OF NON-DOING

Sorry. Non-doing and wasting time are not the same. Vegging out in front of the TV or Instagram is wasting time. Non-doing is the opposite. It's mindful. Clearing away the clutter of the mind— which anyone who does it can tell you is heavy lifting—and paying attention to everything as a means of staying in the present.

"The most precious gift we can offer anyone is our attention," said Thich Nhat Hanh, a Vietnamese Buddhist monk who helped bring the concept of mindfulness out of the monastery and into the world, including Google's HQ, where he is a frequent guest speaker. Mindfulness is a branch of meditation, and everyone from Oprah to Gwyneth Paltrow talks up its benefits. The United States Marine Corps offers mind fitness training to help soldiers de-stress and increase emotional intelligence. And big corporations like Nike offer employees classes on, of all things, how to just sit and do nothing. Which in our hyperstimulated, hyperdistracted world might just be the only way back to yourself.

THE CONSCIOUSNESS REVOLUTION IS COMING!

Consciousness is becoming as ubiquitous as mindfulness. They're not exactly the same thing but are sort of cousins. The idea here is that people are "waking up" and trying to help save the planet by getting together and spreading kindness and goodwill. Although, consciousness is a very subjective term, as pretty much anyone would say that they are the conscious one and that other people are not. Who decides? To get a little more far out, certain boho circles believe that when the Mayan Calendar ended in 2012—actually not the end of the world but just the end of one of its Great Cycles—humanity left the Piscean age and entered into the Age of Aquarius. Change is coming, and it is up to us to become "conscious" and adapt and evolve. And to help with this formidable challenge are such offerings as the conscious media network Gaia, a sort of Aquarian Netflix with thousands of "consciousness-expanding" films and documentaries such as *Connecting with Universal Consciousness* and *Secrets of the Pineal Gland*. The coworking space the Assemblage, in New York City, is for the conscious capitalist, and bills itself as "a community of individuals who believe the world is on the verge of a collective conscious evolution, transitioning from a society defined by individualism and separation into one of interconnectedness." Then there are the crypto consciousness symposiums in places like San Juan, Puerto Rico, and on the Greek island of Mykonos that address tipping this new technology into the positive.

NEUROSCIENCE IS COOL

The scientific study of the nervous system is nothing short of a boho obsession. Neuroscience legitimizes spirituality and ancient practices by using a language that the mainstream respects and understands. When I replace the flaky term "vibe" with the authoritative "frequencies of the hippocampus," people seem to pay more attention. Try it.

Over the last fifteen years, the medical view of the brain has changed dramatically with the acceptance of the principles of neuroplasticity—the brain's ability to change as we create new neurons throughout our lives. Accessible MRIs for brain scan research didn't exist until recently. And neuroscience has sought to explain the relationship between the central nervous system, the autoimmune system, and emotional, physical, and mental health. This is where neuroscience connects back to, and undergirds, long-standing spiritual traditions, which in the recent past might've been dismissed as nonscientific at best and mystical nonsense at worst. The Dalai Lama has been instrumental in this collaboration. He began asking researchers who traditionally focused on negative psychology to start investigating the causes of positive emotions. In his book *The Universe in a Single Atom*, he writes, "My confidence in venturing into

Mayan calendar

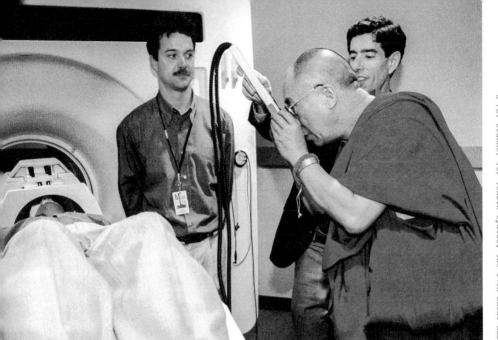

Psychology professor Richard Davidson (far right) demonstrates a PET scanner for Tenzin Gyatso, the 14th Dalai Lama

science lies in my basic belief that as in science, so in Buddhism, understanding the nature of reality is pursued by means of critical investigation."

So next year, instead of going to Coachella, try attending the annual conference of the Society for Neuroscience in Washington, D.C.—or perhaps head to the grand mansion on the outskirts of Berlin that houses the International Forum for Meditation and Neuroscience.

DESIGNER MEDITATION

Most mainstream meditations are based on ancient Hindu or Buddhist practices, like Tibetan Buddhism, which is practiced by the Dalai Lama, or Vedic meditation, upon which mantra modalities such as Transcendental Meditation are built. But I like discovering new hybrids of meditation

introduced by microgurus and upstarts. After all, if appropriation is part of music and fashion—everyone from Madonna to Marc Jacobs does it—why not meditation too? Plus, philosophies like Buddhism are thousands of years old, so it seems appropriate to customize and modernize a meditation practice. I recently met a woman in Mexico who teaches meditation on stand-up paddleboards in the ocean among dolphins—I suppose if no dolphins show that day, then that becomes part of the meditation? There's Kundalini Disco, developed by DJ Amy K., who blares disco hits while leading kundalini mudras, breathing, and meditations to reach nirvana. No cocaine needed. And Hugging Meditation, prescribed by love guru Sasha Cobra, where pairs do just that for extended periods of time.

At the Habitas hotel, Tulum, Mexico

"The energetic connection produces oxytocin (the 'love' hormone), reducing stress and social anxiety, while rebuilding confidence, self-assurance and self-love," Sasha writes on her website.

Biet Simkin, a former musician and heroin addict who started the Center of the Cyclone, leads her meditation experiences onstage at the Bonnaroo festival, at the galleries of the Museum of Modern Art in New York, and at NeueHouse, a coworking space in New York and Los Angeles. Biet said she developed her signature technique—part hatha, Vedic, and Zen, plus her own emotion-inducing music and breathwork—for stressed urbanites who are into fashion and beauty and don't want to live in a monastery. Rather than calm down and detach, "I think it's more effective to learn through the heart," she told me.

Neurofeedback meditation will appeal to science-minded life hackers. I haven't tried this, but I'd really like to. The concept, developed in the late 1950s, is that experienced meditators (people who have been practicing for more than five years) are able to synchronize brain waves in the alpha and/or theta range—the zone of calm and tranquility. Beginners have trouble reaching this plateau. But they can mimic this state, the theory goes, by using a small iPod-sized EEG (brain wave) device that runs wirelessly on a computer. You place tiny sensors on your head, and the device's software analyzes your brain waves in real time.

When you've successfully synchronized the alpha and theta brain waves, you're rewarded with a pleasing tone.

HEAD TRIPS: JOINING THE GOOD-VIBE ARMY

Meditation studios are becoming as common as gyms in progressive cities around the world. (Some coffee shops offer meditation, though truth be told, caffeine doesn't always mix well with mindfulness.)

In New York City, Inscape, a yurt-shaped dome lit in nightclubby purples, is on the more luxury end of the spectrum. And in Portland, Oregon, the minimalist Pause Meditation is where serene,

Inscape meditation studio, New York City

bright-eyed groups gather for sessions lasting from thirty to ninety minutes.

You can also find your meditation tribe on the go, without a fixed studio to call home. Roving groups of enlightenment hunter-gatherers meet up in loose-fitting clothes to meditate in people's homes (the schedule dictated by when the host gets home from trekking in Nepal), art galleries, back gardens, lofts, parks, and even department stores.

The real reason to go to a meditation studio is for the community of like-minded (or like-mindful) souls. Your social inhibitions are broken down, and instead of engaging in nervous chatter, you'll often find yourself having meaningful exchanges about deep emotional states and existential issues. In the après-meditation zone of vulnerability and openness, sincerity tends to shine through. And it sure beats happy hour or another feckless night on Tinder.

That said, be prepared for anything: *do* brush your teeth beforehand, and wear clean socks.

THE GONG SHOOK the thin walls of my sparse dorm room. It was 5:15 a.m. and still dark out. I pulled on my sweatpants and a baggy T-shirt, per the monastic dress code, and joined the other yogis in the dining hall. We had all vowed "noble silence," so the only sound from a hundred yogis hunched over the long institutional tables eating oatmeal and stewed prunes was the gentle clanking of spoons. It was day 2 of the meditation retreat at the Insight Meditation Society (IMS) in the hills outside the small country town of Barre, Massachusetts, where they practice Vipassana, a branch of Buddhist meditation also known as the Thai Forest Tradition. I had enrolled cold turkey, having never meditated before other than a handful of sporadic eleven-minute attempts while propped up uncomfortably on sofa cushions in my living room.

I felt I had to do something radical. I had reached an energetic impasse in my life, practically paralyzed by self-doubt and fear of failure that were affecting both my professional and personal lives. Sometimes a whole weekend would pass, and I'd be stuck in a reddish-brown chamber of doubt and loathing, glued to my smartphone, which of course only made it worse. It didn't happen all the time, only when certain insecurities were triggered. I tried to deal with it on my own—with exercise, yoga, travel, adventure—but nothing worked for long. In fact, it seemed to be getting worse. My Buddhist therapist suggested a stint at IMS. He said learning to meditate might help temper the ups and downs by teaching me to stay in the moment and acknowledge, not react. I figured there was nothing to lose by trying it, although it might be a long week of suffering. The Buddha himself taught that suffering is the path to non-suffering. I could deal with that. I mean, how bad could it be?

When I arrived at IMS, a big brick compound surrounded by rolling fields and forest, the rules were explained by a volunteer worker, a slight young man with electric eyes and a goatee: no talking, no eye contact, no reading or consumption of any type of media. For sure no sex. The daily schedule was forty-five-minute blocks of seated meditation in the big hall bookended by thirty minutes of walking meditation until the final gong at 9:45 p.m. There was also breakfast, lunch, and a bowl of soup and crackers for dinner, a chore (mine was sweeping the hallways; I had narrowly avoided being assigned to cleaning the toilets), and one lecture given in the evening, known as a dharma talk. Every other day, we met briefly in groups of eight with the teachers in small conference rooms, and we were allowed to ask a question or two—not more.

Much to my surprise, the seated meditations were the easy part, once I figured out a way to stack the cushions into a little stool with blankets under my knees. The rest of the program was grueling. But there were trails in the woods and country lanes, and I would take long walks every afternoon and sing and talk to myself to keep from losing my mind. I was so bored that I found myself looking forward to the ginger salad dressing. I would go out to the parking lot and find my car, talk to it, and stare at my daughter's toys in the backseat. For amusement, I read the license plates of the other cars—New Hampshire: Live Free or Die; Rhode Island: The Ocean State—and also the ingredients of my trail mix. Of course, the boredom is in itself another feeling to acknowledge, and when you do, the mind clears and you can go deeper. Knowing this did not help at first.

Then on the third day, it happened. A breakthrough. During that morning's sit, I was finally able to accept the stillness and boredom. A portal opened, and euphoria flooded in. It felt like having psychedelic orange sunshine for blood and air, and it filled my arteries, lungs, and head. I was smiling so hard and for so long that my face hurt. The "I," the "you," and the "me" all merged. But on Day 4 during the afternoon meditation, I was consumed by fear—a purple abyss—my heart racing, tears streaming down my face as I plunged into a free fall. I forced myself to stay with the fear, which was the realization that I couldn't protect myself or the people I loved, particularly my daughter. I had reverted to a vulnerable little girl, completely freaking out, alone and scared.

I tried to sign up for an emergency private session with one of the teachers, but all the slots were taken by other desperados. So I set out on a five-mile trail, and almost immediately I was laughing uncontrollably and the orange sunshine from day 3 returned with even greater euphoric force. That evening during the seated meditation, I actually fell in love with myself. I apologized to me for being cruel and negligent for so long. It was as if iodine had been poured on my soul and the issues that were buried and gnawing bubbled to the surface and were finally vented after decades of denial. I felt a sense of release and calm.

Still, there were two more days to go. The minutes crept by. I broke the rules and started reading a book about blockchain technology that I had smuggled in my luggage. And finally the seventh day came. I drove back home to New York City elated, either because the retreat was over or because of my newfound inner peace. Or likely both. And funny things began to happen. In a crowded subway, I let everyone go ahead of me until I realized it was too late to get on the train. I cried when two siblings were reunited in a cheesy Disney movie I watched with my daughter. I was more compassionate toward people in my life—without actually trying—and bundles of tension melted away. I've been meditating most days, and I do feel better. And most important, I've come to regard self-love like other relationships. It needs constant work and attention.

MEDITATION RETREATS: CHECKING IN/ OUT

Walking meditation at the Esalen Institute, Big Sur, California

Join the ranks of serious meditators—the kind who sit on a subway with their eyes closed and don't notice anything, or the ones who seem unflappably content and refreshed regardless of stress and bad news. But first you must learn how. Meditating requires commitment, and it can be a grueling process. It's easier if you're in the right setting with the right group. Here are a few options.

Esalen Institute, Big Sur, California

The birthplace of the intellectual New Age Movement in the 1960s, Esalen is both a spa and an educational center. Its outdoor natural sulfur hot tubs perched on the Pacific Ocean are legendary (and clothing is optional), furthering the deep sense of healing here, along with the organic gardens that supply the kitchen. Progressive scholars and the renegade intelligentsia give workshops and lectures. Some Silicon Valley techies invested recently, but the mission, they say, remains the same.

Insight Meditation Society, Barre, Massachusetts

Founded by the meditation A-team of Sharon Salzberg and Joseph Goldstein in the 1970s, this comfortable but simple retreat center in central Massachusetts teaches Vipassana, a branch of Buddhist meditation, with silent retreats led by heavies such as Jon Kabat-Zinn and Salzberg and an occasional visit by His Holiness the Dalai Lama. (Some of the teachers headed west in the 1980s and set up the philosophically similar Spirit Rock in the bucolic hills of Woodacre, California.) Sign up early or get wait-listed.

International Dharma Hermitage of Wat Suan Mokkh, Thailand

This sprawling Buddhist monastery in the forest of southern Thailand is where hard-core aspirants meditate alongside the resident monks. "Guests" sleep on concrete beds with a straw mat and a wooden pillow (gulp!) and have twice-daily chores. Sessions last ten days.

Kripalu, Stockbridge, Massachusetts

A favorite of high-maintenance New York City and Boston enlightenment seekers, Kripalu is a large, well-funded yoga and wellness center with cushy spa-like accommodations and facilities. The meditation programs, taught by in-house and visiting teachers, last a manageable two to five days.

Las Pirámides, San Marcos La Laguna and San Andrés Semetabaj, Guatemala

With two locations near Lake Atitlán, this relaxed meditation center focuses on the cosmos and alchemy. Amenities include meditation temples, pyramid-shaped cabins, a medicinal plant garden, and a communal kitchen. Students are welcome to come for a day or several months.

Mii Amo, Sedona, Arizona

This luxury wellness center and spa is located among the southwestern red rocks and beneath the starry sky. Meditation practice is combined with spa treatments, private consultations, transformational workshops, energy healing, and Native American rituals.

Omega Institute, Rhinebeck, New York, and Blue Spirit, Costa Rica

Started in the 1970s by a Sufi mystic, Omega Institute is an educational retreat center with a Buddhist slant and tons of workshops including on mindfulness, yoga, and psychology. One of Omega's founders started Blue Spirit, an affiliated center on the beach in Nosara, Costa Rica, that offers yoga and meditation retreats.

SELF-HELP SOCIALITE

Went vegan
after watching
Cowspiracy

Sends Rumi quotes
to her mother on
her birthday

Carries
jar of
natural
narcotic
honey that
her friend
brought
back from
Nepal

Oversized
luggage filled
with good-vibe
crystals

Rewrites
wedding
vows with
her husband
yearly on the
blockchain

Italian camping
cot for vision
quest outings
with her shaman
in the jungle

Alpaca
shawls
from trip
to Machu
Picchu

Goop
slip-on
espadrilles

Smartphones
have
radiation-
blocking
cases

Jenny Deveau and Seth Misterka of Dynasty Electrik performing a sound bath

SOUND BATHS

In the airports of Cancún, Mexico, and San José, Costa Rica, you can usually spot a tanned type with salty tangled hair and a waft of lemon oil mixed with BO hauling travel cases holding gongs and metal singing bowls. Sound baths are ubiquitous on the boho circuit—particularly at birthday parties, or gatherings, or date nights—and they are only getting more elaborate. In Berlin, I was invited to a tantric sound bath at the studio of artist Olivia Steele (she's the one behind the road signs in places like Ibiza and Burning Man that say "Breathe" and "The Only Way Out Is Thru"). In Tulum, I attended a psychedelic sound healing hosted by the musician Lum. In Bali and Goa, nearly every hotel on the beach offers a sound bath in a tent or on a roof to demarcate the sunrise or sunset.

Part of why sound baths are so popular is that they are meditative but much easier than meditating, and they activate parts of your brain that are often neglected. Sort of like getting a mind massage. Usually, you lie down on a mat, eyes closed, in a circle with a group. And then the sound healers come around and bathe you with the vibrations of their arsenal of instruments, which can include a didgeridoo, crystal and metal singing bowls, a hammered dulcimer, an African kalimba, rainsticks, and chimes. The sounds wash over your energy field and, ideally, calm the mind. If you're having trouble sleeping after a stressful day, try an evening sound bath instead of a nightcap. Good vibes and even better dreams await.

SHAMANS ON SPEED DIAL

The word *shaman* originated with the Tungus in Siberia and means "one who sees in the dark."

Shamans are the link between earth and heaven. As explained at Monte Albán, a pre-Columbian city in Oaxaca, Mexico, that I visited recently: "It was believed that man descended or sprouted from a tree. Wise healers or shamans were able to communicate with the gods by ingesting fermented juices of plants such as mezcal agave, mushrooms, peyote, and marijuana."

Modern shamans don't necessarily live deep in the Amazon, although it's totally fine if they do. I met a shaman in Alto Paraiso, Brazil, who catered to a celebrity clientele and was dating a model. Another shaman was a clean-cut Parisian with a six-digit social media following whom I met at a loft party in New York. He gave me his business card. Some modern shamans apprentice for decades in the Amazon, collecting plants and learning from locals. Others study under gurus at ashrams in India. There

is no one path. A following and the gift to heal are as close as it gets to an Ivy League diploma.

Shamans offer wisdom and advice in different ways. I met a fashion designer in Valladolid, Mexico, who consults with his shaman on trending silhouettes. And some shamans don't ask you to ingest anything, instead working on an energetic level through massage and ceremony. Your most trusted shaman might officiate your wedding or helm other important life events such as a birth, a conscious uncoupling, or a conversion to Buddhism.

DATING YOUR SHAMAN: PROS AND CONS

DATING YOUR SHAMAN is sort of the boho equivalent of dating a rap star or a pro athlete. If you date a shaman, you'll likely be their assistant for a few months or years, which entails everything from setting up the ceremonies and answering email inquiries to arranging vine-gathering excursions to the Amazon. (What self-respecting shaman is glued to their smartphone?)

Shamans are usually middle-aged men—although increasingly more are women. A friend of mine went to an ayahuasca ceremony in Topanga Canyon and ran into her old Cornell University classmate Jen, who was now sporting a white robe and grown-out blond highlights, answering to the Sanskrit name Jagruti, and doling out barf buckets. But don't enter into this arrangement thinking it's all about the sex. Many *ayahuasqueros* refrain from intercourse for days or weeks—possibly months—before and after the ceremonies to retain their "vital energy." However, they will likely dive into your consciousness—a sort of next-level emotional foreplay. If you're going to date a shaman, remember: Inner beauty comes first.

MODERN SHAMAN

Hair has a natural glow as he never uses shampoo and often swims in waterfalls

Faraway eyes from a steady diet of ayahuasca and witnessing the beginning of time

Faded tattoo from former incarnation as lead singer of a punk band

Necklace has piranha teeth and feathers collected during apprenticeship in the Amazon

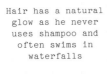

Beaded medicine pouch contains organic almonds and dates in case of a blood-sugar dip

Speaks compellingly about the need to let go of "the narrative"

Hands out feathers as business cards

Wears logo-free clothing

ENTHEOGENS: THE FAST TRACK TO ENLIGHTENMENT

"Entheogens" is the term that the hard-core use for plant-derived psychedelics taken for spiritual purposes, not just going to the EDM tent at Coachella. Bohos don't take drugs; they take "medicine," which implies healing, not hedonism. In other words, don't call ayahuasca a drug. Spirituality is the opposite of being a junkie, even if the truth is that abuse of "medicine" is happening in the scene. The point is, swallowing spiritual and ritualistic psychedelic plants like ayahuasca, peyote (a cactus mainly from the Mexican Desert), or iboga (bark grown in West Africa) is not for the wannabe trap queen.

These psychoactive plants are held sacred for a reason. Meltdowns are a hazard of the trade. Not to mention the barrage of metaphysical questions that will furrow the smoothest of brows. But this is exactly why people try these psychotropic substances in the first place, ideally under the tutelage of a real shaman.

"These sacred plant modalities are difficult paths that are lined with tests," according to Don Howard Lawler, a *curandero* (healer) from Peru. "The tests go specifically to your very weaknesses. The whole point is to help you strengthen your weaknesses and grow from that point on. What this results in is an exceptionally fast pace of personal development and evolution of consciousness. That process is facilitated as much by how you do it, where you do it, and why you do it as by the plant itself."

It's like a shot of enlightenment that might otherwise take years of dedicated, intensive meditation to achieve. But it does wear off. So it's not surprising that many people, after trying hallucinogens, get heavily into meditation because they understand clearly the power and thrill of working with the mind.

Most psychedelics are illegal in the United States. Some, such as peyote, psilocybin mushrooms, and LSD, are Schedule 1, the "most severely restricted," because they are deemed the most addictive with no accepted medical use by the U.S. Drug Enforcement Agency (DEA). In many states, marijuana is also Schedule 1, which is clearly a politicized classification because of the proven medical benefits of the drug. Although, cannabidiol (CBD), the nonpsychoactive component of marijuana, was recently reclassified by the DEA as a Schedule 5, the least restricted. And there is growing research that LSD and psilocybin also have medical benefits, as Michael Pollan argues meticulously in his bestselling book *How to Change Your Mind*.

AYAHUASCA

This hallucinogenic Amazonian vine used by indigenous peoples in South America has become the "it medicine" of the modern spirituality movement because it helps connect you to yourself, nature, and beyond. Ayahuasca ceremonies, presided over by a shaman, have groups of people gathered in various locations: retreat centers, converted old churches, nightclubs, or a home somewhere in the countryside.

You can tell who the regulars are because the area around their cushions is tricked out with scented oils, feathers, talismans, and favorite pillows. Fashion and sexuality are played down here. Do not show up in tight jeans. Instead wear loose-fitting white clothing. The ritual is referred to as a "sit." As in "I sat with Xander in Guatemala last week." Also, you might overhear someone say, "He 'drinks,'" usually considered an endorsement. Ayahuasca is a tool for you to access the center of your being without the static and white noise. You also become one with the vine itself, its DNA, and all the wisdom it holds. This respect for plants and Mother Nature is particularly needed right now.

THE AYA-RIVIERA

For true ayahuasca immersion, go closer to the source. Ayahuasca retreat centers abound in Costa Rica, Brazil, and Ecuador. But the epicenter is in Iquitos, Peru, a sort of aya-Riviera in the rainforest. ("Aya" is the nickname given to the vine.) There in the fecund jungle, where ayahuasca vines are native, are the telltale palm-thatched compounds.

The retreats run from a few days to a few weeks and cost between a couple hundred dollars and a couple thousand. (Many retreat centers have websites, but nothing beats word of mouth for a solid recommendation; you should always be discerning about whom you "sit" with and where.) The centers tend to be backpackerish with basic huts, but many have on-site farms and organic food. There are several resident *curanderos*, and it's often a family affair, with a grandfather, Don something, and his sons and grandsons (and occasionally a nephew and a cousin) brewing their own batches of ayahuasca on-site. They boil the ayahuasca vine and leaves of chacruna, a plant that contains the psychedelic compound DMT, in pits of water and then combine the two into a dense brew.

During the ceremonies, which usually happen at night and last about six hours, the shaman sings *icaros* (sacred songs) and plays instruments to help channel frequencies from nature. And the cosmos.

TIME LINE: ENTHEOGENS ENTER THE MAINSTREAM

1910s

Occultist and author Aleister Crowley begins experimenting with peyote and conducting rituals. References appear in *The Drug and Other Stories* and *The Equinox*, Volume 3 No. 1, and in his performance piece *The Rites of Eleusis*.

1930s

Jean-Paul Sartre takes mescaline.

1952

Beatnik William Burroughs, interested in telepathy, clairvoyance, and getting wasted, travels to Panama, Colombia, and Peru to "score" ayahuasca. His findings are published as a series of letters to Allen Ginsberg known as "The Yage Letters." "Yage may be the final fix," Burroughs concludes in his novel *Junky*.

1954

Aldous Huxley's book *The Doors of Perception* recounts his experiences on mescaline.

1957

R. Gordon Wasson, a vice president at JP Morgan, publishes an article in *Life* magazine, "Seeking the Magic Mushroom," about his journey to the mountains of Mexico and his time with María Sabina, an indigenous Mazatec shaman. Beatniks head south in search of a similar experience.

1960

Two young psychologists, Dr. Timothy Leary and Dr. Richard Alpert (aka Baba Ram Dass), launch their Harvard Psilocybin Project.

1960s

Carlos Castaneda publishes three books on his "apprenticeship" in the Mexican desert with a Yaqui Indian peyote shaman.

1973

Terence and Dennis McKenna publish *The Invisible Landscape: Mind, Hallucinogens, and the I Ching.*

1962

Iboga is marketed in France as a stimulant called Lambarene. (It's declared illegal and withdrawn in 1966.)

2006

The United States Supreme Court gives the small religious sect UDV (the full name is O Centro Espirita Beneficente União do Vegetal), based in New Mexico, the right to keep importing ayahuasca from South America.

2016

The New Yorker publishes "The Drug of Choice for the Age of Kale: How Ayahuasca, an Ancient Amazonian Hallucinogenic Brew, Became the Latest Trend in Brooklyn and Silicon Valley" by Ariel Levy.

2018

Michael Pollan's book *How to Change Your Mind*, about the medicinal benefits of psychedelics, becomes a bestseller.

IT WAS MY first ayahuasca ceremony. A shaman, an American ex-fashion stylist who had studied for years in the Amazon, was presiding at her house in upstate New York. My friend Ana was supposed to go with me but couldn't make it. Now I had ten days to secure a cohort—no easy task, as most people don't flippantly sign up to spend a long night puking and excavating the recesses of their mind. I had met Carlos—a Colombian artist-type living in New York City—exactly once at a party, and he seemed to share my penchant for edgy exploration. I liked him in a way I hadn't felt about anyone in a while and wanted to get to know him more. Ingesting ayahuasca was a risky first date, hardly dinner and a movie. Allen Ginsberg described the experience as "a big wet vagina" or "great hole of God-nose." A friend of mine calls it "liquid love." I wanted to confront my inability to see my own power. I was finally ready, after years of clever avoidance, to take a hard look beneath the shiny surface, one that I had worked so diligently to keep polished and impermeable. In fact, I wanted the surface to be blown right off, venting whatever might be shelved underneath. There was also a real possibility that I'd be reduced to a frothing rabid animal, thrashing around on the floor screaming and crying, my hair caked in puke, tearing off my shirt, shitting in my pants, or freaking out in some other unbecoming way that had been described by my friends. But I emailed Carlos anyway and held my breath. His response: "Absolutely. I believe I am very ripe for the experience. Count me in."

The day of the ceremony was a sunny June morning, fresh with new leaves and potential. Carlos met me at a café in Greenwich Village, and we drove a couple of hours north until the concrete gave way to a vibrant blanket of green. Carlos had never taken ayahuasca before either, and so the flirtatious dynamic typical on first dates quickly morphed into one of practical and brave camaraderie, as if we were on a survivalist expedition, both of us giddy and nervous about our imminent plunge into the deep end. Carlos talked about his divorce—he was in the middle of dissolving a ten-year marriage. I told him about a recent breakup I was recovering from and said I was trying to regain my balance.

At around 5:00 p.m., we arrived at an old stone mansion. It looked like a forgotten relic from another era, with stained-glass windows, a sagging roof, and ancient lopsided trees. Several other cars were already parked there. We carried in our bags, which held a change of clothes, a toothbrush, and some groceries for breakfast. As instructed by the shaman, I had also brought a sleeping bag and a pillow. Inside, the grand parlor room was adorned with ornate moldings but had few furnishings, mainly just floor cushions that at this moment contained about half a dozen dazed Ukrainians with aerodynamic haircuts (there had been a ceremony the night before, and they were staying on for round two).

By now any anxiety I had over impressing Carlos had morphed into fear about what was going to happen to me. I went into the bathroom, with its soaked and moldy bath mat, and changed into my ceremony clothes—a white kurta that I had bought for Holi festival in Jaipur, India, a few months earlier and silk pajama pants, my attempt at ayahuasca chic. Carlos managed to look elegant in a blue T-shirt and navy cotton trousers. I actually fell a little in love with him at that moment, mainly because he had been hardy enough to come on this adventure with me. The shaman appeared in loose clothing. She had just woken from a nap, her long curly hair tousled. She hardly spoke except to tell us to keep the ceremony top secret so as to not endanger the community. I had made a list of intentions and issues to address. I asked her about them, and she just smiled and nodded. I understood that this was to be the extent of her guidance. She said she was exhausted from the previous night and needed to conserve her energy. She was an "aya-monk" and had forsaken alcohol, sex, and many types of food for several years.

Just after sunset, it was time for the ceremony to begin. The shaman's assistant, a chiseled, handsome man, called the group up to the attic. At the top of a narrow staircase was a long rectangular room with low-pitched rafters. Eighteen mats with lavender sheets had been set up in neat rows on each side with "purge" buckets in front, and at the end was the shaman's altar, denoted by an array of instruments and talismans. Carlos and I found two empty mats near the altar. The shaman had changed into a regal Amazonian outfit: an embroidered tunic, her arms and neck draped with necklaces and feathers. She invited us up one by one to "drink the medicine." I kneeled in front of her and was handed a shot glass filled with a lumpy brown liquid. My body convulsed at the taste: earthy and alive. Carlos took his gulp and we looked at each other: "So long. Good luck." Then I totally forgot about him.

I lay down on my mat with my eyes closed. The ayahuasca was kicking in, but I decided to hold off on my intentions for a while and just enjoy what was happening. It was the right choice. Textures and tunnels and delightful vine-shaped worlds emerged, playful and light. I was smiling and began tracing the contours of my cheekbones in a blissful oneness with my body and spirit. I heard swishing noises as the shaman came past with burning sage and feathers to wisp the smoke. Instruments began to play, and she was singing in a strange tongue and pitch. I was off, deeply in my mind. Eventually, I opened my eyes.

I felt totally sober. Carlos's eyes met mine, and we smiled. I wanted to hold him—elated that we had made it this far in one piece—but it was hard to move. He reached out and held my hand. The warmth sped through my body. We snuggled into each other and whispered about our trips and giggled. The shaman offered the group another round of medicine—for those who wanted to "go deeper." I went up. I still had my list of intentions to address. This time the trip was more intense. I presented my intentions and "it" teased me. "It" was the center of my mind or an ancient spirit, or likely both. "You tourist," it taunted. "You don't just ask. You have to let the journey unfold to get your answer." So I backed off. And then it finally said, "All of your questions have the same answer. And you know what it is." It was true; I did.

At around 4:00 a.m., the shaman turned up the lights. The ceremony was over. We trickled downstairs and lay on the mats in the living room. Some people were hungry, so Carlos went into the kitchen and cooked frittatas. We sat on the terrace under the stars and had existential, semicoherent conversations. My body and mind were exhausted. I was lost in the beautiful peaks and valleys of Carlos's accent—but I was too weak to sit up, so I crawled up to the attic, curled up in my sleeping bag, and fell fast asleep. When I woke up, Carlos was asleep on the mat next to me. I felt a profound connection to this man. It was deeper than attraction; it was an appreciation and love for his mind, for his willingness to take a chance, to journey into the unknown. Not only was he unafraid to stare at the truth, but he solicited it. Imagine how far we could go together in overthrowing the rules and creating something new and beautiful.

As we drove back to the city, we were like old friends. We talked about meandering instead of taking a linear path. About cosmic crumbs. He told me he didn't believe in love or relationships anymore. I didn't want to hear it. When things fell apart eight months later, it was seemingly impossible to get him out of my head. The idea of him—and of us—was implanted deep in my being, down the winding viney path where the ayahuasca had led me. It was a painful and arduous process to go back in and dig him out. So the moral of my story: maybe dinner and a movie is a better idea for a first date.

THE PSYCHEDELIC REVIVAL: BEYOND THE ACID CASUALTY

Timothy Leary in front of the Hitchcock mansion, Millbrook, NY, circa 1968

In 1960, two young psychologists, Dr. Timothy Leary and Dr. Richard Alpert (who later changed his name to Baba Ram Dass), launched the Harvard Psilocybin Project to explore how psychotropic substances affected the human mind. Student volunteers ingested LSD and psilocybin—both legal substances at the time. Leary and Alpert were fired three years later (for taking the drugs while conducting experiments and for promoting it for recreational use, among other things). LSD quickly became the counterculture party drug of the decade, and by 1970, Congress had banned all psychedelic use.

Richard Nixon called Leary "the most dangerous man on earth." And let's be honest, there were a lot of acid casualties when this potent psychedelic was gulped down by the vial load by hippies who'd stay high for days or longer (check out the Merry Pranksters documentary *Magic Trip* to watch footage of how a person can lose their mind and "get off the bus" permanently).

Although there was considerable medical research being done with LSD before the Harvard Project, after the drug became a symbol of rebellion against society, it all came to a grinding halt. But over the past decade, the scientific community has resumed research on LSD and psilocybin. LSD "reverses the more restricted thinking we develop from infancy to adulthood and could pull the brain out of thought patterns seen in depression and addiction through its effects on brain network," according to David Nutt, a professor of neuropsychopharmacology at Imperial College London who conducted imaging studies of the brain on LSD and psilocybin. In addition to helping people with depression, anxiety, addiction, and PTSD, they have also been shown to have benefits for healthy people. According to a 2006 Johns Hopkins study, taking the drug even one time can fundamentally reshape lives, making people happier and kinder, more productive, and more open-minded. (For more on the therapeutic benefits of LSD, read Michael Pollan's insightful 2018 bestseller, *How to Change Your Mind*.)

In the 1960s, the standard LSD dose was an over-the-moon 250 micrograms (and many people took a lot more); in the early 1980s, it dropped down to a more restrained 100 micrograms. These days, people take a fraction of that, which is symbolic of the neo–Age of Aquarius. Experimentation often works better in moderation. If there is a lesson to be learned from the '60s, let it be that.

MICRODOSING

Bohos swear by microdosing (taking one-tenth of a full dose of psychedelics like LSD and psilocybin). They are interested in self-improvement, not self-annihilation, and science has made it possible to trip under specific and controlled circumstances.

James Fadiman introduced the term "microdosing" to the mainstream in *The Psychedelic Explorer's Guide* (2011). The idea originated with his friend Albert Hofmann, the Swiss scientist who invented LSD in 1938. Hofmann was a proponent of microdosing and described the practice as "the most under-researched area of psychedelics." He took what is thought to be the first intentional

PSYCHONAUT

Grown-out highlights after cutting all exposure to cosmetic chemicals last year

Sand in pockets left over from last week's solar eclipse in the Mojave Desert

3D-prints her clothes in psychedelic patterns

In folder is a prospectus for investing in a Swiss biotech start-up that's doing research on clinical LSD

Bag stuffed with serotonin-replenishing foods (bananas, figs, plums)

Sleeps on floor mat to stay in contact with the earth's electric energy

Worn huarache sandals in homage to author Carlos Castaneda

Currently reading:

Pihkal: A Chemical Love Story by Alexander Shulgin and Ann Shulgin

Breaking Open the Head: A Psychedelic Journey into the Heart of Contemporary Shamanism by Daniel Pinchbeck

LSD trip in 1943, and microdosed throughout the last couple of decades of his life. (He died in 2008 at the age of 102.)

The whole point of microdosing is to enhance consciousness, not achieve unconsciousness. It's the opposite of getting really drunk.

Some ambitious upstarts take a capsule of dried magic mushrooms with their breakfast before work every morning to gain a competitive advantage in the workplace. (According to *Wired* magazine, "the practice induces a 'flow state,' aids lateral thinking, and encourages more empathetic interpersonal relations.") Steve Jobs famously said, "Taking LSD was one of the most important things in my life."

Ayelet Waldman, who wrote the book *A Really Good Day: How Microdosing Made a Mega Difference in My Mood, My Marriage, and My Life*, microdosed LSD every third day for a month to help her with acute depression. "I feel happy," she writes in *A Really Good Day*, after taking her first LSD dose. "Not giddy or out of control, just at ease with myself and the world. When I think about my husband and my children, I feel a gentle sense of love and security. I am not anxious for them or annoyed with them. When I think of my work, I feel optimistic, brimming with ideas, yet not spilling over."

CHAPTER 2

FREE LOVE

Type A Yogis,
Polyamory, and
Tantric Unicorns

A conventional marriage is akin to house arrest on a suburban cul-de-sac.

Challenging societal norms is sport for bohemians. Especially when it comes to sex and relationships, as any boho would agree. Instead, consider something not so locked down, like your version of polyamory. This is where it's good to date within the same circles so someone with traditional notions of the patriarchy doesn't clip your wings. Date night is a handful of sex dust and a tantric workshop or maybe a poly sex party or a platonic cuddle puddle where you explore new sensitivities. If you're single, well, let's just say there are *a lot* of options.

And if you do marry, weddings, officiated by a shaman or an eccentric friend (or an eccentric friend who is a shaman), are held at Burning Man, with the bride in a glittery white bikini and silver platform boots.

The body and the mind work together to reach enlightenment. Or at least, they have to stop working against each other so much. The conventional limits we set on our bodies, and our morality, just hold us back from our physical and spiritual potential. Yes, you have to be (somewhat) responsible. However, before you embark into the depths of free love, you must learn to love yourself. (It takes training.) Which is why the first stop is yoga.

YOGA: THE GATEWAY DRUG

Yoga is a form of meditation that is also exercise. When I went to my first yoga class, I refused to chant or sing in Sanskrit because I thought it was corny. I just wanted a workout! But slowly, my mind and body began to work together, and the rhythms of the chants made sense. Lift a leg—breathe in. Lower the leg—breathe out. Make space to go deeper into Warrior Two. I did. And I started noticing that I could make space for other things in areas of my life where I thought there was no room and no

flexibility. Now I'm the one chanting along loudly in my off-key voice. I even found the courage to lead a few yoga retreats (see page 48). Meditating came next. The same breathing as yoga, the same concentration, only this time the effort is on focus—or, as my galactic maestra friend Serita says, "flowcus." It's actually harder because there is no movement to align the breath with. I was up to fifteen minutes a day, five days a week. Then I went to a weeklong Vipassana silent meditation retreat (see page 20). Before I knew it, I was sprinkling turmeric on broccoli, rubbing lavender oil in my armpits, and spending Saturday night in a sound bath.

ASHTANGA TO YOGA RAVES: FINDING YOUR INNER YOGINI

It's not a question of *if* you practice yoga but rather *what kind*. The type of yoga you practice says a lot about who you are. Are you a type A neurotic? Chances are you're into Ashtanga. Would you describe yourself as a high-endurance cuddler type? Then AcroYoga is probably your jam. Luckily, there are tons of different styles of yoga, from the classics offered at chains like YogaWorks, to the far-out cultish, to the extreme sport. And if none resonate, why not create your own?

MAINLINE YOGA

The following primary traditional types of yoga are mostly hybrids of hatha from India. They came to the West starting as early as the 1950s, and got more popular with the dawning of the Age of Aquarius.

Ashtanga: Founded by K. Pattabhi Jois in the 1940s, Ashtanga is a fast series of poses aligned to breathing. To this day, its hard-core devotees will spend a month studying at Jois's Ashtanga Yoga Research Institute in Mysore, India.

Bikram/Hot Yoga: Founded by Bikram Choudhury in the 1970s, this type of yoga is for those who like to feel as though they are actually practicing in a hot, crowded studio in India, even if they're really in a onetime sweatshop near their office in SoMa or SoHo. Heat cranks up to a sauna-like minimum of 105 degrees with 40 percent humidity.

Iyengar: Precise poses are held for long periods and often modified with props. In the 1970s, B. K. S. Iyengar founded the Ramamani Iyengar Memorial Yoga Institute, in Pune, India, which still operates a study center and is a coveted stop on the yogi trail.

Kundalini: On the sexier end of the spectrum, the meditations, mantras, and strenuous pose-holding practiced by this school of yoga are intended to release the kundalini (serpent) energy in your body. U.S. practitioners include disciples of Golden Bridge Yoga; many of the teachers and students wear white tartans.

Tantric: Practitioners will insist that it's less about sex and more about harnessing the five forces of Shakti, the female deity who represents creativity and change. A popular pose includes the yab-yum, in which the smaller of the two partners sits cross-legged on the lap of the other.

EXTREME YOGA

For adrenaline junkies not content with confining their practice to a mat.

AcroYoga: This is a hybrid of acrobatics, healing arts, and yoga. You work with a partner. One person stands or lies on the ground and balances the other using his feet and hands to hold her in the air while she attempts various yogic poses like handstands and backbends.

Aerial yoga: Yogis use antigravity hammocks and silks (usually in purple

TANTRIC YOGI

Exhales in long,
moan-like sighs

Carries
breast-
massage oil

Meditates in the
middle of parties
when energy is
too much

Has armpit
hair; loves the
smell of her
own pheromones

Wears her yoni egg
while practicing

Tight shredded Mad
Max—style crop top
doubles as daywear
on the playa

Dog-eared copy of
*The Enlightened Sex
Manual: Sexual Skills
for the Superior Lover*
by David Deida

Scrap of paper has
info for class on
sacred snake dancing

and/or other hippie circus colors) as props that aid the body in positioning and alignment. You do a lot of hanging upside down, which decompresses the vertebrae of the spine. Some devotees claim to gain up to an inch and a half in height.

Slacklining: Created by rock climbers as a way to improve balance when landlocked in a courtyard or condo. Now yogis are deriving pleasure from attempting crow pose atop a thin strap of rubber suspended in the air.

OUT-THERE YOGA

Today's gurus sport athleisure wear and have dreamed up countless modern hybrids of yoga. Here are a few.

Cannabis: Finally, a class you're actually supposed to come to stoned. Held mainly in states where marijuana is legal, the first half hour is the "stoner social" where people vape and share joints (according to Dee Dussault, who teaches a ganja yoga class in San Francisco), followed by an hour of yoga. Participants are invited to stick around after class for thirty minutes to sober up. Brownies optional.

Laughter yoga: Forced laughter soon turns into real and contagious heaves of joy. Twenty minutes of laughter is said to be sufficient to achieve full physiological benefits.

Nude: Everyone in class is buck naked as a means of celebration and removing layers of inhibition. No staring. Or if you want to cop a peek, do it when no one is looking while in downward dog or a handstand.

SUP yoga: Yo, it's yoga—not for bros, but atop a stand-up paddleboard. A new offering in the water sports category.

Yoga raves: Glow sticks, pink-dyed hair, and sun salutations at 130 beats per minute. Hit up the bar afterward for energy mocktails.

A PRETTY GIRL wearing a floral-print bodysuit asked me how to get down to the beach. You could see the beach right at the bottom of the hill below our rented villa, and there was a clear path down. "I don't know," I said, shrugging, wondering why she (1) was asking me, and (2) was asking such an obvious question. And then I remembered. It was because I was leading the yoga retreat. Along with an actual yoga teacher from Venice Beach, I was in charge of a group of fourteen women and one boyfriend who had trekked from Los Angeles, New York, and Boston to Careyes, a remote and idyllic resort community on the Pacific Coast of Mexico, for a week of soul-searching and sun.

Being the leader was a major experiment for me. I'm a writer, sometimes an entrepreneur, sometimes a designer—nothing remotely close to a healer or nurturer. Before I had my daughter a few years ago, I didn't even have a houseplant to take care of. That was how I liked it. I'm used to working and traveling on my own. I go on solo surf trips, and I'll happily travel alone to faraway countries where I know no one. A favorite sport of mine is to go on journeys to practice what I call "social self-reliance" (which can be harder than a desert crossing). Like when I went by myself to Mykonos recently and plopped right into the middle of the hectic summer party scene with no friends and few connections. I like the discomfort of having to convert strangers to friends and navigate environments based solely on how charismatic or interesting I can be in that moment. Often I fail.

Now I wanted the opposite challenge. On the yoga retreat here in Mexico, one of my jobs was to "take care of" the students. Empathy doesn't always come easy for me, but I vowed to try my hardest. Every morning, our group woke just after dawn and hurried over to an open-air yoga studio perched in a jungle with wild vines and palms. Afterward, we gathered for brunch on the shaded terrace of our yellow-painted villa. The discussions got deep; the students—from housewives to hedge fund managers—opened up about problems ranging from stalled-out marriages to feeling "dead inside." Anxieties, insecurities, diarrhea—nothing was off–limits, especially after a few days, when everyone had gotten to know each other. Our meals became like informal self-help workshops. At first, it made me uncomfortable to share such intimate details with strangers, and worse, to have them look to me for advice. I pretended that I knew what I was doing, and soon I sort of did.

Sunset was the time for rituals—the yoga teacher led a meditation on an island accessed by a rope footbridge suspended hundreds of feet above the rocky ocean. In the Copa, a giant bowl-shaped structure the size of an amphitheater, an artist from New York City built a fire and had us write things we wanted to "get rid of" on pieces of paper and toss them into the flame. Being a leader, I decided I'd better come up with a ritual too. So I had the idea for a laughing symphony. I was the conductor and stood in the middle of the group and waved my arms around like a crazy bird indicating when the group should laugh at high or low pitches. Even though it was a half-baked and maybe ridiculous concept, everyone played along in a show of support. I was touched that they were willing to be vulnerable for my sake. By the end of the week, we had been transformed into a close circle of friends. One of the students said I had inspired her to learn to surf. Another said she wasn't afraid to get a divorce anymore. In fact, she was looking forward to being on her own and wanted to travel, sort of like me. I felt helpful in a way I wasn't used to. Turns out I like taking care of people. Although I'm still not very good at the hand-holding stuff like giving directions to the beach.

ASHRAMS: THE GREAT PILGRIMAGE

Before the word was co-opted for boutique hotels, coffee shops, and Burning Man camps, "ashram" referred to a no-frills meditation center, usually in a village somewhere in India. Ashrams became fashionable in the 1960s when many hippies followed the trail to India—including the Beatles, who practiced Transcendental Meditation in Rishikesh under the supervision of spiritual guru Maharishi Mahesh Yogi.

The town, located in the foothills of the Himalayas, still has tons of ashrams, almost always the domain of a bearded guru or swami who in the 1960s wrote an influential but indecipherable book—which you will be encouraged to buy at the reception desk. Unlike plush yoga retreats, ashrams are for the serious. Be prepared to wake up at dawn, scrub dishes in the community kitchen, and forsake coffee, alcohol, sex, onions, and anything that is remotely considered a stimulant. Days are spent practicing rigorous asanas (postures), meditation, breathing (pranayama), cleansing, chanting, mauna (silence), pooja (worship), and kirtan (sacred singing). But this is exactly what it takes to develop a formidable meditation practice. And soon you will be so deep in your psyche that external annoyances won't really bother you anymore. In fact, you will probably start to like the routine. It's a complete reset.

Accommodations are basic and cheap and enforce the devout pilgrim vibe with cot-like wooden beds, bare fluorescent lightbulbs, "cardboard" towels, and a 10:00 p.m. curfew. Minimum stays range from a few days to a few months, so best to quit your job now.

YOGA BE-INS

Part Coachella, part marathon, yoga be-ins are for the hypersocial who get a rush from practicing yoga with hundreds to thousands of like-mindeds. The daylong immersions—organized by groups like Wanderlust—take place in city parks or resorts with DJs, live music, and meals of locavore fare. Wanderlust hosts monthly be-ins in places such as Berlin, London, and Los Angeles. The day starts with a 9:00 a.m. stretch, a five-mile run or walk, and yoga and meditation sessions throughout the day. Boho pro tip: Wear smudgeproof mascara and Aztec-print leggings, and bring a tarot deck as a conversation starter.

SNAG (SENSITIVE NEW AGE GUY)

Can be found at
"clothing optional"
BBQs in Ojai

Used Kickstarter
to fund meditation
app, "Feeling Me"

Asks permission
of flowers before
picking them to
wear in hair

Low-cut
embroidered
vest

Plays the sitar
during jam sessions

Has a crush
on Yoko Ono

Burns palo santo
during romantic
evenings at home

Speaks in a calm
voice even when
stressed or angry

Holds hugs for
a long time

TYPE A YOGI

Likes to take selfies
in challenging poses

Practices yoga every
day except on Saturdays
and during full moons
or new moons

After class,
changes into
power suit
for board
meeting

Lotus
flower
tattoo on
sacrum

Backstage pass
given to her by
rock-star classmate

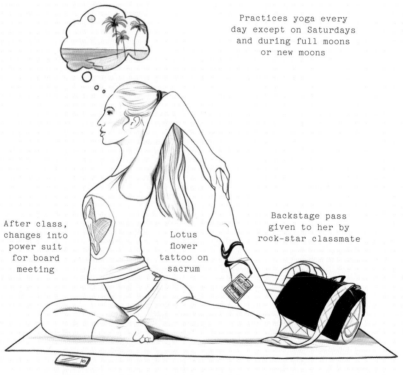

Studied Ashtanga
last winter in
Mysore, India, and
wears T-shirt with
logo of its guru,
K. Pattabhi Jois

Bag is filled
with pins for
her charity,
Breathe for
Water

KUNDALINI YOGI

Prefers natural
high of breathing
exercises to alcohol
or drugs

In keeping with
Yogi Bhajan's edict,
wears white turbans,
kurtas, and tunics

Flirtatious
twinkle in eye

Marigold-colored
rope bracelet,
a souvenir from
the rigorous
Bihar Yoga School
in northern India

Canteen is filled
with chai and
Moon Juice's
Sex Dust

Uses the terms
"kundalini rising"
and "serpent energy"
as compliments

Sheepskin is faux

SPORTY YOGI

Does yoga between Soul Cycle workouts

Necklace pendant says Ohm

Lives in Spiritual Gangster athleisure wear

Ubers to yoga class

Saved up to treat her three besties to a week at Canyon Ranch

Does sit-ups during Shavasana

Designer sneakers

TRAVELING YOGI

Peruvian scarf is a gift from a healer she met during the lunar eclipse in Cusco

Sneaks in Tree Pose while waiting in line for the bathroom

Dabs lavender essential oil on cute guy in the window seat

Crystal pendant necklace is used as a pendulum for making decisions

Yoga mat doubles as a camping mat

Is Zen about people cutting in the security line

WhatsApp is filled with the first names of "friends" (guys in beach towns from Puglia to Nosara, where she hosts yoga retreats)

DANCING THE GYM ECSTATIC

COMBINE DANCING WITH yoga, and it's cross-training with benefits for the aura, not to mention free-range legs, an Ibiza-style tone that you can't get at even the fanciest gyms. The more you dance, the sexier and happier you will feel. My advice: the crazier the dance, the better. If you are self-conscious and dance only halfway crazily, it looks silly. But when you really get into it, the appeal is undeniable. You become magnetic. So close your eyes, smile, and throw your heart into it!

The power of spinning around and jumping up and down to reach a hypnotic trance state is well known by bohos. Especially sober ones. Ecstatic dancing (also known as 5Rhythms or conscious clubbing or kundalini clubbing) is done at alcohol- and drug-free gatherings, often rave-type events held in big concert venues in cities around the world. They might kick off with a cacao ceremony and a yoga warm-up session and end with a gong bath. The goal is a high-octane, occasionally spiritual workout to rev up the endorphins au naturel.

Daybreaker is an organization that holds ecstatic dance raves in cities from London to San Francisco between 6:00 and 9:00 a.m., before the workday starts. Massage trains emerge spontaneously on the dance floor—there's lots of smiling, patchouli oil, slinky athleisure wear, and butt cheeks spilling out of metallic hot pants.

DO	DON'T
Dance as wildly as possible	Grind on a stranger's leg
Bring a water canteen	Bring a plastic bottle
Smize (smile with your eyes)	Talk on the dance floor
Show up to the office afterward with a dusting of glitter in your hair and a (naturally) wired smile	Give a full-body hug if you are dripping with sweat

POLYAMOROUS COUPLE + UNICORN

Unicorn pendant made of gold and white diamonds, a gift from the first couple she dated

Sunglasses on top of head in case night turns to dawn

"Dom" bob haircut

Manicured goatee

Leopard-print choker. Meooow!

I'm with Them

Pilates-toned arms

Prefers pom-pom socks to lingerie

Platform boots to add height

Snug leather pants (can see package)

Faux-leather dress

She met the poly couple at Burning Man's Robot Heart party dancing at the sunrise session

He keeps a stash of Adderall, Xanax, and Viagra in his pocket

All three wear triple-heart infinity rings, a group Valentine's Day present

POLYAMORY IS THE NEW NORMAL

You can be in more than one relationship, with full transparency and the support of everyone involved. Some polys are married and take on outside lovers— a practice known as hierarchical polyamory—more common if there are kids involved, or a mortgage. But there are other ways: some polys live in a house with their partner and their partner's other partner(s) and possibly a few kids— so-called family-style polyamory.

A couple I know from Los Angeles who married in their early twenties are now ten years older, have two young children, and are bored sexually. But they love each other and don't want to break up their family. So instead of getting a divorce or having exhausting and hypocritical secret affairs, they took on an older couple (cool, with, as it happens, their own plane and yacht) as occasional lovers. The happy quad attended music festivals like Envision in Costa Rica. It lasted for a year. Sometimes polyamory works out, sometimes it works for a while, and sometimes, despite the best of intentions, it doesn't work at all. It's the effort, and the commitment to experimentation, that counts.

The central idea of polyamory is honesty and trust—nothing freaky there! In fact, honesty is supposed to be more important than sex. *Supposed to be.*

Unlike swingers—the 1970s term for coked-up married couples who pick up other couples in the hot tub—bohos, with their constant need for a scientific basis for their behavior, have familiarized themselves with studies done on human mating and psychology that question accepted notions of monogamy. Most bohos devote a section of their library to such dog-eared tomes as Dossie Easton and Janet Hardy's 1997 gospel, *The Ethical Slut*, and *Sex at Dawn* by Christopher Ryan and Cacilda Jethá, which draws on primate physiology to prove that monogamy isn't even for the birds. Not even penguins. (They're monogamous only for the mating season.)

GET ON IT: BOHO SEX TERMS

conscious lover

"Conscious lover" is a term I first heard from Bibi Brzozka, a sacred sexuality and tantra teacher. It means a lover who is "aware" and tuned in to their second chakra. For men, that would mean moving past friction-based sex with the goal of ejaculation. Most important, foreplay should last for an hour because they know that's how long it takes for women to get properly stimulated. For women, it means being able to summon feminine energy and receive and to be cool with a semi-erect penis. A conscious lover takes their cues not from porn but from a real energetic connection. Both parties go within and are responsible for their own orgasms. They use breathing as an enhancer. Lovemaking sessions clock in at four hours on average.

sex magic

Harness the mystical power of sex. Start with an intention-setting ritual: Sit facing each other in candlelight and begin an eye-gazing meditation. Or put your foreheads together and breathe, imagining a white light surrounding you both as you become one. Then the manifesting will start, and you might be amazed where it will lead.

sex positive

Open-minded and kind of just into everything. Poly, bi, unicorn, but also responsible and ethical, which means they practice safe sex and are "consent aware." The most common boho sex subset, being sex positive means you're the kind of person who takes your partner out for vegan brunch after a drug-fueled S and M orgy one day and the next day might be getting your yoni stroked for 120 minutes by a tantric masseur in Copenhagen. Not you? Never say never. That would be so bourgeois.

unicorn

This cute and cuddly staple of children's cartoons and mythology has been co-opted by bohos to describe a horny but pure young beauty running free in a magical land of dating apps and orgies. The connotation is that this unicorn is not only single and hot but also part of a rare breed that wants to have sex and be in a relationship with a couple—probably one that's married and older and can give them entry to the high life.

yoni and lingam

Learn the dialect of the sex positive. A boho would not use pornishly conventional terms like "wet pussy" or "hard cock." Instead, make a more enlightened impression in the bedroom (or yurt) by using the ancient Sanskrit words *yoni* (vulva, or "sacred space") and *lingam* (penis, or "shaft of life").

TANTRA

Lovers in Dalliance, eighteenth century

Tantra is sex, meditating, slowing down, and elevating your consciousness all in one cheerful activity. It's the belief that sexual energy can help you be more connected to yourself and the world. The key, of course, is learning the art of tantra—"to loom or weave" in Sanskrit. But learning can be fun! Especially this type of learning. Tantric Hindus worshipped the deities Shiva (the auspicious masculine one) and Shakti (the divine feminine) and believed that enlightenment is reached by joining these forces. One could say we are in a tantric societal moment. Men are collectively accessing their feminine sides, as evidenced by dads becoming hands-on parents and the ≠metoo movement, which is questioning old power structures and behaviors. In order to evolve, women and men need to work together harnessing and harmonizing their priorities.

In tantra, sex becomes a meditative process. Men retain ejaculate so as not to deplete vital energy and also to feel more invigorated afterward. (Being able to control explosive and implosive orgasms is called "sexual continence.") Women not only can have orgasms as they are not depleted by them, but they can have six different types, including the thunderbolt (or *sahajoli*) and the nipplegasm (or *shyama puja*). For both genders, the channeled energies coursing throughout the body raise the level of sexual consciousness and consciousness in general. Ideally, a spiritual or higher plane is reached. Nirvana!

TANTRIC PICKUP LINES

CONSCIOUSNESS IS SEXY, so you'll need pickup lines to match. Try these with a sincere tone while gazing at the person's aura, not their ass.

~~~~~~~~~~~~~~~~~~~~~~~~~~~~

» Your energy is so pure

» You are . . .
  * a goddess
  * a high priestess

» We are . . .
  * from the same star galaxy
  * ancient lovers

» I've loved you in a past life

» I'd love to . . .
  * give you a sound bath
  * give you a massage
  * be in your auric field
  * serve you
  * visit your crystal palace
  * introduce you to my shaman
  * be in ceremony together

~~~~~~~~~~~~~~~~~~~~~~~~~~~~

TANTRA RETREATS

Looking to respark your relationship? Forget the all-inclusive hotel in the Caribbean; get freaky and try a tantra retreat. Maybe go to Ko Pha-Ngan, Thailand, and attend a workshop such as "Tantric Rituals That Will Help to Create a Deeper Bond Between You and Your Partner, That Will Make Her Feel Like a Goddess." Go as a couple or by yourself. But if you go solo, there are no assurances that you won't get paired up with a weirdo. So, writes Vilhelm Kruse, a tantric coach who runs TantraVaerkstedet.dk in Denmark, "If you want to be completely sure that your future soul mate is the right size, height, and sex, then please bring your own partner. Other than that, we advise you to surrender to the choice of the universe—surrender to whoever is present with an open heart. If you are lucky, you'll meet your own beautiful self." BYOP (bring your own partner) and BYOS (bring your own sheets).

Many tantra practitioners have followings and hop around the world hosting workshops at various resorts and healing centers in liberal enclaves. Some retreat centers are specifically designated for tantra. Others, although tantra is offered, are buried under the banner of yoga—as tantra and yoga are of course closely related, and also, it wards off the pervs. Here are some retreats to check out.

Agama Yoga, Ko Pha-Ngan, Thailand, and Rishikesh, India
Heavily rooted in the yogic traditions of hatha and kundalini, Agama offers a range of tantra classes, such as the weeklong "Serpent Power Retreat," "Evolving Through Tantra," and "Conscious Conception."

Coravida, Quepos, Costa Rica
An ecoresort with tree-house guest rooms that doubles as a "conscious community" with a focus on tantra workshops given by a variety of teachers, including the well-known cofounder Shaft, a "Sacred Sexual Awakener" and tantra sex coach who teaches people how

to achieve orgasms, heartgasms, and breathgasms. His workshop "Tantricorns Dance into the Bliss" sounds interesting.

Ibiza Tantra Festival, Ibiza, Spain

Held every October on the idyllic isle of Ibiza, this festival is the Sundance of the tantra community, drawing a who's who of tantra and offering an orgasmic array of workshops and talks.

Pachamama, Nosara, Costa Rica

This alternative off-the-grid ecocommunity in the jungle isn't exclusively tantra, but it does offer several tantra workshops. Founded by a disciple of Osho, it embraces the sexual ideals of the guru's teachings.

Solluna Tantra, Ko Pha-Ngan, Thailand

Shashi Solluna is a leader in the Taoist school of sexual arts and tantra. She guides people to activate their root sexual-creative energy at retreats that she leads around the world, with a concentration in Ko Pha-Ngan.

Source Yoga, New York City, Santa Cruz, Los Angeles, and Big Sur (at Esalen)

Charles Muir, a coauthor of *Tantra: The Art of Conscious Loving*, creator of the "Sacred Spot Massage" and many other experiential exercises, founded this tantra academy in 1979. It offers roving seminars around the United States.

Tamera, Southwestern Portugal

This peace research village and commune was founded by a group of German progressives in 1995. The Love School promotes the community's core belief that peace comes with ending the war between genders. Down with jealousy and in with truth! Courses include "Ethics of Free Love" and "Free Sexuality and Partnership."

Tantra Heart, Ko Pha-Ngan, Thailand

The Tantra Heart consortium hosts its brand of young, inclusive tantric retreats at a secret jungle resort.

THE NEW PERSONAL TRAINERS: SELF-LOVE COACHES AND SEX GURUS

Nobody wants to do it wrong, especially when it comes to Eastern sex practices. What an embarrassment it would be to stroke the upper clitoris for an hour when the most nerve endings are in the central region. Or to be hunting for his frenulum and instead happen upon his urethra. It would be like trying to get to Paris, France, and ending up in Paris, Texas. But it's not just about technique. It's about getting rid of technique, deprogramming ideas of sex that we've largely been conditioned to believe because of porn and media. Is getting banged on the kitchen counter for ten minutes better than connecting energetically and spiritually for hours and having full-body orgasms? Get a sex guru or self-love coach such as Sasha Cobra or David Deida and sign up for a weekend retreat.

ORGASMIC MEDITATION

The idea here is that if a woman's clitoris is stroked for a while, she'll reach an orgasmic state (not to be confused with a climax, which lasts for only a few seconds) that will elevate her consciousness and thus improve her life. While this has long been an aspect of tantra, the concept was refined and marketed by OneTaste—founded by entrepreneur Nicole Daedone, the author of *Slow Sex: The Art and Craft of the Female Orgasm*, in San Francisco in 2004—which now offers classes around the world, from Los Angeles to London. The company's signature is a fifteen-minute orgasmic meditation (OM) practice in which women lie down in "nests" of pillows and get their clitorises stroked by (usually male) "research partners" wearing latex gloves. According to OneTaste, the clitoris has seven different areas, each one offering nuanced emotions when stroked (sort of like foot reflexology).

OneTaste ran into some problems recently when a group of former staffers accused the company of brainwashing and manipulating them into maxing out credit cards to buy classes and expensive retreats. Despite the controversy, no one seems to dispute the powers of orgasmic meditation itself.

YONI GEAR

Crystal Wands
No plastic straws, and no plastic dildos either! The crystal "wands" are usually made out of rose quartz, the stone of the heart and unconditional love. I like the marketing terms used by popular brands such as Goddess Wand and Chakrubs: "higher awareness," "conscious self-pleasure," and "spiritually nourish."

THC Lube
Now yonis can get high too. Weed lube is actually not a lubricant per se but cannabis oil blended with liquid coconut oil. It is applied topically and takes twenty to forty minutes to work. It is said to promote relaxation and blood flow where you want it. There's also a THC and CBD rectal suppository for men. Fun for everyone!

Yoni Eggs

A staple of Asian cultures, these jade eggs are inserted in the vagina to strengthen the pelvic floor. The eggs were popularized by Gwyneth Paltrow, who sold them on Goop until a lawsuit ordered her company to pay a $145,000 fine because its claims—that yoni eggs regulate periods and correct hormonal imbalances—were not backed by scientific evidence.

Yoni Steams/V-Steaming

Wombs are believed to be the cauldron of power, and yoni steams are a ritual to clean the sacred womb energetically of past lovers and other impurities, and to promote the discovery of our depths. Boil herbs such as mugwort, rosemary, calendula, wormwood, and holy basil in water and squat over it. Or you can order a yoni steam box on sites like SteamyChick.com.

1. He is a bio-hack coach and guru.
2. She is a Daoist tea ceremony giver/goddess and harp player.
3. He wears Circadian Lifestyle sandals.
4. She goes barefoot.
5. All lights are amber toned to keep the cortisol down and the melatonin up.
6. Instead of champagne, he serves live spring water in a flute glass.
7. Foreplay is tantric breathing followed by an eye-gazing meditation (takes four hours).
8. Aphrodisiac herb garden in window box
9. Chinese wedding bed—a couch is too traditional
10. Framed sacral chakra poster
11. On coffee table, *The Power of Now* by Eckhart Tolle and a bottle of erotic essential oil
12. A Solaris healing blanket (a gift from one of his students), developed by the Russian space program to shield from EMFs

- They met in a cuddle puddle at a Halloween decompression party in Topanga.
- He likes her aura. She likes his paleo wolf energy.
- They trade sweet nothings about their shadows playing and the inner work they are doing.
- Later on, he shows her his new infrared sauna, which is installed in the bathroom.

CANYON LADY

PORTRAIT OF A
MODERN-DAY BOTANIST

Kari Jansen, owner of Poppy & Someday, at
her home studio in Laurel Canyon, California

YOU CAN EASILY tell how boho someone is by the type of deodorant they wear. Was it bought in a chain-store pharmacy and does it contain aluminum? (Not boho.) Or was it bought at a health-food chain like Whole Foods and have no aluminum? (Semi-boho.) Or! Did it come from a small-batch goddess purveyor type who forages her own herbs during the full moon? (Legit boho.) No deodorant at all? (More hobo than boho.)

And it doesn't stop at the armpit. Chic and beautifully branded alternative apothecaries catering to pagan goddesses have popped up everywhere from Marin to Missoula. Shelves are stocked with body salves made of bergamot, goldenseal, and maybe a touch of CBD oil, organic plant-based remedies, and earthy tinctures in thoughtful, sustainable packaging.

Many of the products are made by independents working out of their home, like Poppy & Someday, a natural beauty company in a house at the top

of a winding road in the Laurel Canyon section of Los Angeles. It's run by herbalist and single mom Kari Jansen, who has a sprawling herb garden in which she harvests her own cypress, copal, and lavender. In the middle of the garden sits an old-fashioned claw-foot bathtub where clients soak in the nude during treatments, their long hair spilling out over the lavender shrubs. Kari does all her mixing and packaging out of her garage. Products include Marfa Moon Mist, Spirit Weavers Syrup, and, of course, deodorant.

The corporate patriarchy should take note. Women don't want your products or your shame anymore. We can simply head out to the forest and make our own—or get them from friends, or friends of friends, who do. We'll be taking care of ourselves now, thank you.

CHAPTER 3

THE SOCIAL SAFARI

Gypsetting, Turbans,
Burning Man, and
Festival Hopping
from Bali to Brazil

Dancing at Coachella in Moroccan tunics, sun-bleached hair still salty from surfing in Malibu

the day before—it might seem, at least if you follow some of the more dedicated adherents to the boho lifestyle on Instagram, that they are always somewhere sublime, or perhaps jetting off to a yoga retreat in Costa Rica and then, happily centered and before June brings the regular tourists to spoil the Mediterranean vibe, they are lounging topless (no visible tan lines) on the rocks in Formentera.

Travel is part of the boho DNA. There are so many festivals now that it's possible to exist in an alternate reality, hopping from one to the next. And since you can do your work anywhere (see Laptops in Paradise, page 164) and Airbnb your place back in Clinton Hill (Brooklyn) or Capitol Hill (Seattle) while you're away, why get stuck in some commuter rut when

you can go on a voyage that is also one of self-discovery? Although bohos are inspired by the hippie ideals of the 1960s, this time around, traveling is done not with a ratty backpack but with an indigo roll bag, a rose-gold MacBook, and a cyberwallet stuffed full of bitcoin.

It's not that you avoid luxury, but being pampered is not that important. Bohos want an experience that upends their understanding of themselves and frees them from the individuality-keeping regimens of consumerism. Which could mean sleeping in a tree house, taking night walks with a local astronomer, or maybe traveling to the laid-back coastal Moroccan city of Essaouira for a Berber music festival. It's not about fear of the world; it's about discovering it.

MEET THE GYPSET

Remember the jet set? Before global travel became a commodity—and airports felt like a cattle call—these midcentury swells built elite compounds in some of the most beautiful parts of the world. The gypset are different. Instead of a walled-off country club, they want bare feet in the lobby, lounging by the pool in hammocks, meditation classes on the beach, and organic farm-to-table fare. Oh, and really good Wi-Fi to Skype in for meetings back home.

Bohemian to the core, gypsetters are a group of trust-funded artists, broke charismatics, office-averse entrepreneurs, globe-trotting environmentalists, and spiritual seekers who lead seminomadic, unconventional lives. Their approach to life is based more on creativity than on money, inspiration rather than accumulation, but it's not a lifestyle that comes with health insurance or a 401(k), so having a few friends with homes by a good surf break doesn't hurt. Also, it helps if you are French or Brazilian, or at least have a French boyfriend and a Brazilian bikini.

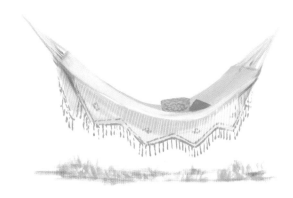

HOW GYPSET ARE YOU?

1. Which "San" would you rather spend time in?
   (A) SAN MIGUEL DE ALLENDE, MEXICO
   (B) SANTA TERESA, COSTA RICA
   (C) SAN QUENTIN, CALIFORNIA

2. What is considered the most prestigious address?
   (A) CENTRAL PARK
   (B) PACIFIC COAST HIGHWAY 1
   (C) GPS COORDINATES

3. Beni Ourain is the name of a:
   (A) BERBER CARPET
   (B) MIDDLE EASTERN RESTAURANT IN QUEENS
   (C) GUY YOU MET AT BURNING MAN

4. You would prefer to vacation in a:
   (A) FOUR SEASONS HOTEL
   (B) YOUTH HOSTEL
   (C) YURT

5. What would you pair with an evening gown?
   (A) CHRISTIAN LOUBOUTIN STILETTOS
   (B) GREEK SANDALS
   (C) BARE FEET

6. Jane Digby was:
   (A) A BEATNIK IN TANGIER
   (B) A BRITISH ARISTO TURNED BEDOUIN
   (C) MICK JAGGER'S FIRST GIRLFRIEND

7. Your alcohol of choice is:
   (A) CRISTAL CHAMPAGNE
   (B) MEZCAL
   (C) AGUARDIENTE

8. It is okay to make your own:
   (A) MONEY
   (B) KOMBUCHA
   (C) BED

9. You would rather join a:
   (A) GYM
   (B) DANCE PARTY
   (C) SILENT RETREAT

10. You get your fashion inspiration from:
    (A) *KEEPING UP WITH THE KARDASHIANS*
    (B) BURNING MAN
    (C) *WILD WILD COUNTRY*

Tally up the points for your score

1. B=10, A=5, C=0
2. C=10, B=5, A=0
3. A=10, C=5, B=0

4. C=10, A and B=0
5. C=10, B=5, A=0
6. B=10, A and C=0

7. B=10, C=5, A=0
8. B=10, A and C=0
9. B=10, C=5, A=0

10. B and C=10, A=0

85 to 100 = You are a true gypsetter. See you at the Mayan Warrior party in Mongolia.

70-84 = You're not a hard-core gypsetter yet, but there's potential. Keep at it!

69 and below = Hopelessly jet set. Enjoy Saint-Tropez.

GYPSET FAMILY

Kohl eyeliner
(belongs to his
girlfriend and worn
Keith Richards—
style). But not for
vanity; it absorbs
the sun's glare.

Vintage 1970s aviator
sunglasses from a
defunct brand, an ironic
statement about reliance
on corporations. Dust
buildup on the lenses
from so many years
going to Burning Man.

Facial hair to
hide chiseled
jawline, his
signature feature
when he was an
Abercrombie &
Fitch model

Edwardian Sgt.
Pepper psychedelic
military jacket,
perfect for formal
events, raves, and
glamping. Custom
made by the same
English tailor
retained by the
Beatles.

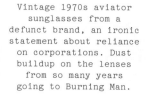

Granddad's
1950s Rolex
Submariner worn
over his tattoo
of the sun

Embroidered
medicine pouch
(a gift from his
personal shaman)

In pouch:
Pens with logos
from various
restaurants and
hotels around
the world

Dog-eared copy of
Joseph Campbell's
*The Hero with a
Thousand Faces*

A few lint-
covered capsules
of melatonin

Italian white
linen pajama pants
(with a monogram
belonging to
the host whose
villa he stayed
at last month in
Sicily). The pants
are useful for
spontaneous yoga
sessions during
layovers at the
airport or in
long lines at the
coffee shop.

Instead of product
in her hair, has
salt from morning
surf session

No worry lines. Not
from Botox but from
a robust meditation
practice.

Vintage coin headpiece
(can also be used as
money in the likely
event of a lost
wallet)

Faded henna
tattoos
leftover from
a wedding she
crashed on a
recent trip
to India

Tahitian black-pearl
necklace (self-
polishes when it's
worn in the ocean)

Natural hemp
dress. Mom's
doula found it in
the hippie market
in the village
of Nimbin,
Australia.

Marks on stomach
from recent cupping
therapy session

Custom meteorite
ring given to her
by a UFO abductee
from Truckee,
California

In backpack:

Passport with
page extensions,
even though she's
only six years
old

Chopsticks, her
preferred eating
utensil

Handmade doll

Fringe on her
denim cutoffs is
from years of
wear. (They were
definitely not
bought that way.)

Cut on
knee from
falling
out of
tree-house
bunk bed

Vintage embroidered
robe that mom got
in the 1960s while
living with a local
horse whisperer
outside Kabul

Free-range legs, toned
by dancing all season
on the beach in Ibiza

Goes barefoot
because of new
study suggesting
health benefits

In mochila bag:

Business card of astrologer
in Rishikesh, India

Universal plug adapter

Poems

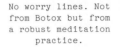
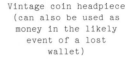

WANDER AND GATHER: TRAVEL TIPS

A few pointers to get you off the couch and on the road—and about what to do once your journey begins.

LAST NAMES

Boho travelers aren't defined by our families or our pasts. We are a self-invented flock; asking a surname sounds like what a networker at a carpeted convention center in Des Moines might do, in order to follow up on LinkedIn later.

In lieu of a last name, a boho moniker is simply a first name amended with the enclaves that said boho frequents. Such as, "Do you know Carolyn from Kenya?" or "I just ran into Brian from Byron Bay." The names can be expanded to include multiple stops on their migratory trail: "You know, Olympe from Panarea, Cornwall, and Lamu." Of course, sometimes a surname must be acknowledged, like in the event of border crossings, hotel reservations, and drug arrests. But then it's best forgotten.

PACK A TURBAN

The far-flung costume party is a boho aspiration, perfected by Talitha and J. Paul Getty Jr. at their Palais de Zahia, the eighteenth-century palazzo in Marrakech where in the late 1960s djellaba-clad rock stars lazed around on daybeds smoking opium. (Not that that went all that well in the end, with Talitha's heroin overdose and J. Paul Getty III's kidnapping, but it sure looked chic.) So when traveling, always pack something festive in the very likely event of an invitation to a spontaneous costume party. It's much more casual than, say, attending one of the Vienna balls. Something small and unique that fits in a carry-on bag will do, like a shell necklace or a pair of slippers that curl up at the toe. The mere act of having one of these sartorial talismans in your possession will further the likelihood of something exotic happening.

WHERE ARE YOU GOING NEXT? "+47° 2' 49.79" N, +102° 42' 28.24" E."

Street names with house numbers are so bourgeois. GPS coordinates, on the other hand, connote a locale—and life—that's flexible, off the grid, and unconstrained by the anti-fun strictures of government bureaucracy. The Genghis Khan Polo & Riding Club in Mongolia, for example, doesn't have an address, as there are no roads there. Drivers just punch in the GPS coordinates—they are the ones listed above—and forge through the grass toward the destination. And when local teens go to town mixers, they exchange GPS coordinates instead of phone numbers, as cell reception is spotty at best. So even if you're not in Mongolia or another remote enclave, it's very boho to use GPS coordinates, including in places like Austin or Philadelphia. Try this on your next dinner party invitation.

AIRBNBOHO

You don't need to be rich to travel all the time. All you need to do is sublet. The short-term leasing of real estate has enabled us all to be temporary Kate Mosses, slumming in remote beach towns like Deià, Mallorca, or Trancoso, Brazil, and it's only getting easier with more and more lodging websites. Thinking about a surf trip on the Pacific coast of Mexico? Do it. It is likely cheaper to sublet your house or apartment and leave town for a month than to stay home. You still have to buy the plane ticket, of course. But you can easily offset that cost plus a week's worth of organic salads and surfboard rentals with your sublet cash. A cool, photographable interior is easy to achieve with a plush Berber rug, some floor cushions, and a few Moroccan wedding blankets nailed to the wall. The bookings will pour in.

ASTROCARTOGRAPHY

Don't be a tourist; be a seeker. Turn off your phone and consult an astrocartographer, who uses your astrological chart to determine the places in the world most aligned energetically with your spirit. The chart won't tell you to do anything specific, like check into the Chateau Marmont. Instead, the astrocartographer will identify your "personal power lines"— several longitudinal energy lines that

correlate to planets like Neptune, Mars, and the sun. Then you can choose any place on that meridian.

For a more detailed consultation, seek out a private astrocartologist, but there are also free computer-generated maps from sites including Astro.com. I tried it, and it turns out my Venus line runs right through Ojai, California. If I were to go there, I could expect this: "An extremely pleasant and relaxing time [where] social life takes precedent, and meeting people is a more harmonious activity."

But if I followed my Mars meridian and went to Merida, Mexico, I could expect this: "A lack in considerateness, patience and diplomatic behavior. Being impulsive can lead to fights and arguments. Lack of levelheadedness can easily lead to accidents and injuries."

Good to know.

THE PLANETARY PILGRIMAGE: FROM FULL MOONS TO METEOR SHOWERS

Of course, sunsets, but also solar eclipses, super moons, comet encounters, and Perseid meteor showers: bohemians have their own alternative calendar of cosmic events that are in tune with the pagan and astrological. The legendary full-moon parties on Ko Pha-Ngan beach in Thailand, now overtouristed, were started by pleasure-seeking bohemians in the 1980s. The full moon is still a reliable, galactic occasion for mushroom tea and dancing all night from Goa to Sayulita. Trekking to the desert with sleeping bags to observe a total lunar eclipse or gathering after work at your local yoga studio when Mercury exits retrograde is also groovy.

Pyramids of Giza, Cairo, Egypt

BOHO SIGHTSEEING: VISITING THE EARTH'S SEVEN CHAKRAS

You saw the Louvre and the Vatican while studying abroad in college. Now that you're a grown-up, your touristic bucket list should include the world's seven major chakras, one on each continent. These places are believed to correspond to the human chakra points and the highest energy vortexes on the planet. Not surprisingly, ancient peoples were hip to this too and often built temples, pyramids, and other worshipful structures there.

1. **Crown chakra:** Mount Kailash, Tibet
2. **Heart chakra:** Glastonbury and Shaftesbury, England
3. **Root chakra:** Mount Shasta, California, United States
4. **Sacral chakra:** Lake Titicaca, on the border of Bolivia and Peru
5. **Solar plexus chakra:** Uluru-Kata Tjuta, Australia
6. **Third eye chakra:** Kuh-e Malek Siah, triple border of Iran, Afghanistan, and Pakistan
7. **Throat chakra:** Great Pyramid at Giza and Mount Sinai, Egypt; Mount of Olives, Jerusalem

IT WAS POURING rain as I checked into Habitas, a glamping hotel on the beach of Tulum. The receptionist, a man wearing kohl eyeliner and beaded necklaces, ran my credit card and then instructed me to get down on the floor and set an intention for my stay. I sprinkled copal on some smoldering coals—a space cleansing—and took a few deep breaths, then made my way to my tent. I had always avoided Tulum because I suspected it would be a bohemian cliché: uptight city people groping for enlightenment over long weekends in luxury hotels. They were there, but I also found something much more interesting. It is a commercialized utopia for an international community of bohemians—or people who are interested in sampling that lifestyle— who prefer shamans to doctors and sound baths to Jacuzzis and can recite the ten principles of Burning Man on demand. Everyone is really friendly.

"It's a social experiment," Eduardo Castillo, an owner of Habitas and a DJ who builds splashy Burning Man camps, told me over juice at the restaurant, a sleek glass-and-steel structure with Moroccan furnishings and a yoga mezzanine. "People come to be part of our family. The hotel is engineered so that guests feel included and make new friends." Indeed, the welcome pamphlet says: "You are now in a place built with the intention to bring you closer to yourself but also closer to others, as you may never know what that next person you exchange a smile with will bring you." For Habitas, luxury is not about palatial digs but about an instant and welcoming community of like-mindeds. Access does have a price tag, though; tents start at four hundred dollars per night.

Tulum Beach, Mexico

Maxa Camp, a Burning Man camp whose founders are a group of young guys from Mexico City, operates a pop-up hotel down the beach from Habitas. You know you've arrived when you see the sign—a vintage black bus parked on the side of the main road next to neon-lit deer antlers. The deer is the camp's logo. It represents the Huichol Indian mythological peyote creature. From there, you walk toward the beach, past a sign in the sand reading "Leave No Trace" and more blue deer sculptures, and find a cluster of brown military-type tents that serve as the glamping hotel. A palm-thatched kitchen is staffed by volunteers whipping up passion fruit cocktails and quesadillas. Pretty women with long tanned legs wander about in fringy kimonos and bikinis; the sun-kissed men have tattoos and yoga-toned torsos. Most of the revenue comes from beach parties with Maxa's in-house DJs, friends, and members of the camp, who have Burning Man followings, and brunches and dinners prepared by an international coterie of chefs. Many of the furnishings—such as the rugs and deer sculptures and tepees—came directly from Burning Man in a shipping container.

A guy called Roberto runs the day-to-day at Maxa Camp, and he explained that they want to effect change and provide a meeting place for people they dub the "Maxa group"—young entrepreneurial types who migrate between Tulum (December–February), London (March–April), Ibiza (May–June), Mykonos (July–August), and Burning Man (late August–September). After September, Roberto said, they rest before starting the rotation all over again.

Nomade is a luxury hotel with some rooms and some luxury tents farther down the beach. (In the high season, oceanfront suites cost around eight hundred dollars per night.) Everyone who can afford it—and believe me, the prices made me blanch—loves it here. Amenities include a wind chime sculpture garden, healing chairs made out of amethysts, and a vegan restaurant with a long communal table surrounded by comfy Mexican chairs and Berber floor cushions. But the hotel is cool, with nonguests coming to hang out. On the beach, people gathered around long luau-style dining tables in the sand, shaded by palm trees, and ate fresh ceviche and taro root salads. Others snoozed in canopied sunbeds draped with macramé. People splashed around in the sun-speckled seafoam ocean; it was a good vibe. I befriended a guy from L.A. wearing a T-shirt that read "Art Sucks." He was going to a conference called "Crypto Psychedelic" at a place called Eden. I wanted to know more, but I was late for my appointment with Minerva, a shaman and energetic healer who came highly recommended. She gave me the best massage I've ever had. She (somehow) massaged the backs of my eyeballs, adjusted my chakras, and at one point took a bushel of damp herbs and ground them into my head. When she was finished, I smelled like a delicious mojito.

I was late getting back to Habitas for the sunset Quetzal-Senso Meditation. I found the group on the terrace above the restaurant. They were all lying down in a circle, so I slipped in while a crew of healers came around and massaged our heads, zapped our chakras with vibrating instruments, and blew a conch shell in our ears. When it was done, I rushed back to my tent to get ready for dinner with my new entourage.

I had been in Tulum only two days but had already collected a group of friends. Gus from Maxa Camp had invited us to try a new restaurant called Wild owned by a London expat who had moved to Tulum after quitting her career as a festival producer. At dinner, around a table in a strange garden of concrete palm trees interspersed with real palm trees, we drank herbal tea and discussed energy vortexes and shamanic trance music. My new friends, a collection of beautiful men and women from France, Norway, Turkey, and California, begged me to stay longer. "It's a full moon tomorrow night," said a Turkish girl in a headpiece who had quit her job at Apple to join the free-spirit migration. "There will be lots of parties and ceremonies." She had a point. And so I WhatsApped the airline and extended my trip, trying to eke out a few more days in this exotic alternative reality.

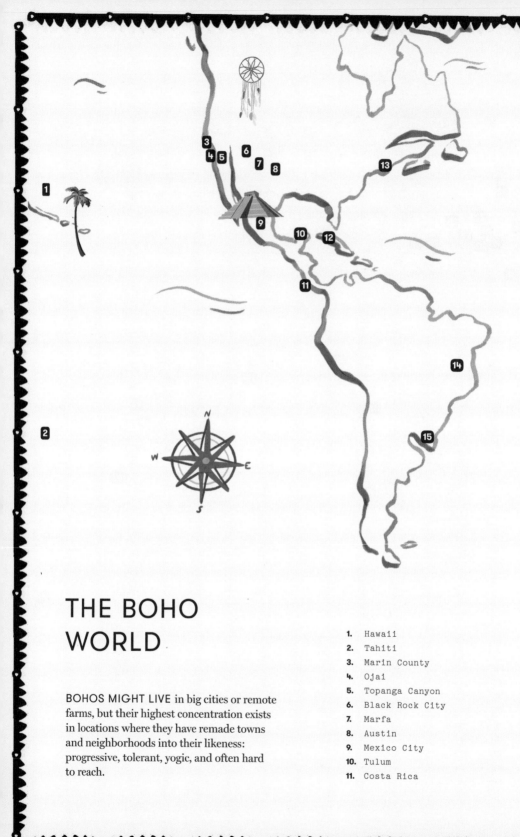

THE BOHO
WORLD

BOHOS MIGHT LIVE in big cities or remote
farms, but their highest concentration exists
in locations where they have remade towns
and neighborhoods into their likeness:
progressive, tolerant, yogic, and often hard
to reach.

1. Hawaii
2. Tahiti
3. Marin County
4. Ojai
5. Topanga Canyon
6. Black Rock City
7. Marfa
8. Austin
9. Mexico City
10. Tulum
11. Costa Rica

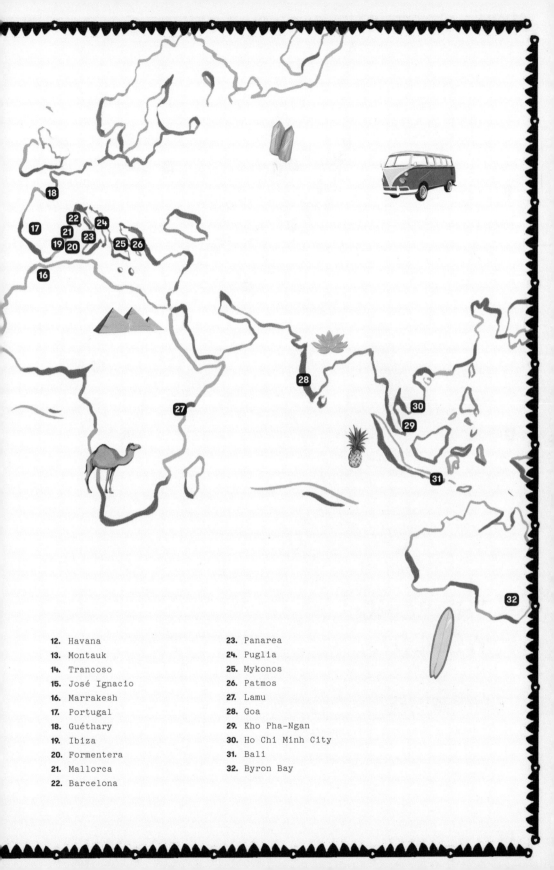

CAFTAN
CLASSIC

Caftans have been a chic staple at least since the 1950s, when fashion designers such as Christian Dior and Balenciaga decided to do their versions of the Mesopotamian garb as a radical reaction to the strict, constructed shapes of that era. In the 1960s, jet-set culture collided with the youthful hippie movement, and the caftan, relaxed yet sophisticated, became its sartorial symbol; *Vogue*'s Diana Vreeland had models photographed in every exotic corner of the globe in bright, billowy caftans designed by Pucci, Pierre Cardin, Valentino, and Yves Saint Laurent. In the 1970s, the glam disco set, including Halston and Bianca Jagger, hopped aboard the trend, and the caftan would never be quite the same.

Simone d'Aillencourt in Pucci, *Vogue*, 1967

His: A caftan adds an instant multicultural flair—and inoculates you against accusations of being a "bro" or "buddy." It's best, of course, if you actually purchased it in a souk in North Africa or Turkey, should you be asked, which you most definitely will. You should only try this look if you're tall. Also: Never pair the caftan with sneakers. Sandals or bare feet work best.

Hers: Caftans originated in the Ottoman Empire. But the most important effect of the Western adaptation is the connotation of abundant leisure, even aristocracy. It is near impossible to do any heavy lifting—let alone the dishes or yard work—in this giant sheath of fabric that engulfs the arms in a billowy butterfly sleeve. The caftan exudes loucheness and is best suited for lying around on a daybed or hosting a cocktail party.

SOUK CHIC

Nothing says bohemian like hand-stitched folkloric embroidery or treasures from the bazaar. They imply at a glance both multicultural reverence and sartorial open-mindedness. Be conscious of the clothes you wear and what they represent.

Huarache sandals

Serape

Incan hat

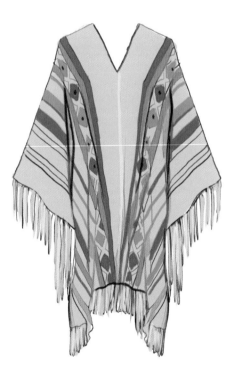

Poncho

Tunic

Mochila bag

Djellaba

Moccasins

Fez

Sunrise dress

Harem slippers

PRINTS
VALIANT

Fabrics are a form of wearable art, showing a sophisticated eye and a commitment to free-form authenticity.

African mudcloth: Traditionally dyed with fermented mud, usually in natural earth tones, with hand-drawn geometric patterns.

Balinese batik: You know a surfer or yogi has spent the season in Bali if they show up wearing harem pants or board shorts printed with the telltale geometric shapes intertwined with nature themes like plants, flowers, and birds.

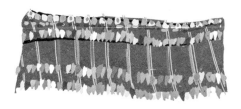

Guatemalan: The gold standard for backpackers in the 1980s and more recently embraced by the fashion crowd, these textiles were traditionally hand-woven by Mayan women in Guatemala.

Ikat: Tie-dye meets the Rorschach test. Ikats have a kind of psychedelic appeal. Extra points for ones with intentionally blurry patterns and trippy mystical motifs.

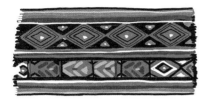

Incan: With a more muted color palette than Guatemalan textiles, these prints come from the descendants of the Inca in the Andes Mountains of South America. Made from local natural dyes—some from insects and minerals—they have a well-traveled patina.

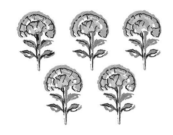

Indian block print: Neobohos love these soft cotton textiles with block prints of lotus flowers, paisleys, and banyan trees, a staple of the hippie era.

Indigo from West Africa: Nothing says "I've been to Mali"—or at least know where Mali is—like this indigo print. Its soothing monochromes of blues and whites exude a minimalist sophistication.

Navajo: Best done in a Native American southwest palette of sunburn and sunrise, the geometric shapes resemble the landscape of mesas and bluffs.

Otomi: A kimono made of a vibrant Otomi would make you a stand out at any full-moon gathering. Made by the Otomi Indians from the Mexican state of Hidalgo, the designs of mythological creatures and nature are said to be inspired by ancient cliff paintings.

FESTIVALS: THE EDM TENT AND BEYOND

A chunk of the calendar is devoted to shacking up in a tepee or RV with several friends to participate in mass music, dance, and art rituals. Festivals are ubiquitous now not simply because people are more into live music but because these ceremonies mark a new belief system. Festivals propose a reality—although sometimes a hypercommercialized one—of community building, crowdsourcing, problem solving, and experimenting with social mores, all while partying and parading around in sexy outfits.

There are the mainstream music festivals like Coachella and Glastonbury and smaller, regional gatherings like Eagle Condor, an ayahuasca meetup in the hills of Brazil. There are so many festivals and microfestivals that you can easily hop from one to the next without ever going home. And many do just that.

THE MEGA FESTIVALS

Festivals like Coachella, Bonnaroo, and Glastonbury pack in upward of fifty thousand people and operate like concentrated versions of the rest of our consumer culture, with name-brand talent, tiered pay-to-play access, VIP no-go zones, and lots of merch. If you can deal with the traffic and high security and the annoying wristbands, it's an easy way to let your boho flag fly, rocking out to the world's most famous musical acts in micro denim cutoffs. VIP passes come at a premium—at least until you get enough likes from the right likers to become an influencer—but as always, charisma goes a long way. Keep smiling, keep Instagramming, and never give up. Explore smaller stages and spend time

Coachella, 2012

at the elixir bar. Fashion photographers from Vogue.com and the latest social media outlets record every lacy onesie, so this could be your big breakout moment.

TRANSFORMATIONAL FESTIVALS

Party with a purpose! Part Burning Man, part wellness retreat, and part TEDx, transformational festivals blend yoga, sound baths, and innovation lectures with bands and all-night DJs. With names like Beloved, Wanderlust, Envision, and Lucidity, these festivals attract the dreadlocks-and-tattoos-on-their-sternums crowd who likely spend winters in a nearby ecovillage—or at least would like to. Musk-scented strangers will walk up and give you massages and full-body hugs. Someone will tie a symbolic bracelet around your wrist. You can learn how to expunge sugar from your diet or ferment noni fruit. The idea here is you leave feeling better, and more enlightened, than when you arrived. Also, there are lots of handouts by the coconut water and kombucha sponsors.

GATHERINGS

Smaller than festivals, gatherings are niche and cater to a specific group, such as the women-only Spirit Weavers, which bills itself as "an embrace of the feminine and ancestral ways," and Herbstalk, for plantophiles. Except for a few late-night guitar sing-alongs, the programming is focused on community building and workshops. It's a chance to really geek out.

THE MOTHER LODE: BURNING MAN

WHEN I SHOWED up at the Burning Man airport, the security guards—volunteer Burners, it turned out—ordered a strip search of me and my friends. I was panicked until the guards themselves proceeded to take off all their clothes and dance around. Another year, I wandered into a dome at the corner of 3:30 and Illusion. A tall warrior-looking man in a tattered Mad Max pilot shirt and dust-caked aviators placed a captain's flight hat on my head and assigned me the task of checking emotional baggage. I stood by the makeshift check-in desk (a card table covered in velvet) and people lined up to write down what they wanted to "check" on a piece of paper and then I tacked it up on a bulletin board. "Regret," "ego," "loneliness": people seemed relieved to get rid of their issues. All out in the open. No therapy needed. This is the sort of experimental mind-set that the world needs more of.

One of Burning Man's missions since it started in 1986 was that the gathering would act like a laboratory to model new and freer modes of human behavior, and, when the annual experimentation was over and its participants returned to their nondesert lives, they would take what they'd learned and change the world for the better. And that's pretty much what has happened. The event's imprint has successfully trick-led out into the "default world" (the Burner term for the world outside Burning Man), influencing everything from business plans to social etiquette, fashion, and, of course, other festivals. The Smithsonian Institute in Washington, D.C., which recently held the exhibit "No Spectators: The Art of Burning Man," called the event "one of the most influential phenomenons in contemporary American art and culture." Writer Daniel Pinchbeck described it as "more decadent than Warhol's Factory, more glamorous than Berlin in the 1920s, more of a love-fest than Pepperland, more anarchic than Groucho Marx's Freedonia, more implausible than any mirage."

There is no money at Burning Man; interactions are based on barter and collaboration, which have become the backbone of progressive business ideas these days. Google founders Larry Page and Sergey Brin, longtime Burning Man habitués, famously prefer hiring Burners to non-Burners. Rules are turned upside down, and conventionalism is subverted and toyed with. People inhabit their fantasies, even ones they didn't know they had. Gifts are given for no reason.

Artists and architects make a pilgrimage to the playa, as the dry lakebed in Nevada is affectionately called, to debut temporary sculptures and installations too edgy and cool (and noncommercial) for the default world. Danish starchitects Bjarke Ingels, a Burning Man regular, and Jakob Lange inflated a giant hundred-foot-tall mirrored sphere called *The Orb*. "The Orb is a mirror for earth lovers—reflecting the passing daytime, evolving life and other artworks beneath it—a new planet to sci-fi fans, a wayfinder for travellers or just a huge disco ball to those who love a good party," the architects wrote. Artist Hank Willis Thomas erected "All Power to the People," a twenty-foot-tall Afro pick that also doubles as a shade structure. And Leo Villareal, who has been displaying his LED sculptures at Burning Man for over twenty years, was recently commissioned to light the Bay Bridge in San Francisco with his LEDs, along with twelve bridges in London, making his work some of the largest public art installations in the world. Talk about influence.

Some years I don't even bother to go to Burning Man because it feels like I've been at the event all year. Burning Man–minted DJ's—and some art cars—rotate between nightclubs, warehouses, and parties from Ibiza to Tulum, San Francisco, Berlin, Los Angeles, and Mexico City. Not to mention actual Burning Man splinter gatherings like Africa Burn in South Africa. My closet now has a growing section just for band leader hats, glittery ice-skating unitards, and Moon Boots.

Most important, the Burning Man ethos (see The 10 Burning Man Principles, opposite) seems to be embedded in our consciousness. It's in our DNA from how we do business, respect the environment, and love each other. At Burning Man–type gatherings—whether it's an ideas festival or a dinner party—people tend to be friendlier ("radical inclusion"), they pitch in ("communal effort"), and they don't leave a mess ("leave no trace"). Finally, it's cool to wash the dishes.

Burning Man now draws over 70,000 people a year, a number that is growing, with tickets becoming scarcer. Some complain about all the tech billionaires in their private planes, the celebrities who come with

The *Orb* by Bjarke Ingels and Jakob Lange

stylies and private chefs, more cops, more stolen bikes. They say the event is becoming more like the real world that they are trying to escape—which is all very true. But the good news is, the real world is also becoming a lot more like Burning Man.

THE 10 BURNING MAN PRINCIPLES

The ten principles were crafted "not as a dictate of how people should be and act, but as a reflection of the community's ethos and culture as it had organically developed since the event's inception," according to BurningMan.org. Regardless, these principles have become a sort of Ten Commandments for bohos—on and off the playa.

1. Radical inclusion
2. Gifting
3. Decommodification
4. Radical self-reliance
5. Radical self-expression

6. Communal effort
7. Civic responsibility
8. Leaving no trace
9. Participation
10. Immediacy

FESTIVALS

	BALISPIRIT FESTIVAL	BONNAROO MUSIC & ARTS FESTIVAL	BURNING MAN
LOCATION	Bhanuswari Resort, Ubud, Bali	Seven-hundred-acre farm in Manchester, Tennessee, with a solar-powered sound system	Black Rock Desert, Nevada
TYPE OF FESTIVAL	Celebrates yoga and "earth-reverent spirituality"	A "friendlier," "crunchier" version of Coachella, with big-ticket musical acts	Not technically a festival, but a community, a temporary city, and an art experience
STAR ATTRACTION	All types of yoga known to man/woman, including Kundalini, laughter, Afro Flow	What Stage (the name of the biggest stage of Bonnaroo)	The giant man that burns on Saturday night
BOHO CRED	Marquee East-West spiritual musicians like Xavier Rudd and Rajasthan Josh	Wear a 1980s Grateful Dead T-shirt to show not-new-to-this jam-band roots	Arriving two weeks early to help build the Temple
OUTFIT	Ripped abs, zero body fat, mandala tattoo on sternum	Topless, covered in body paint	Daytime: as much exposed flesh as possible; nighttime: white faux-fur coat, metallic jumpsuit, moon boots
INSIDER TIP	Come hungry for vegan and veggie fare from kiosks like Alchemy and Bali Buda	Instead of taking a shower, hit the Splash-a-Roo slip 'n' slide area	Bring Xanax, earplugs, and condoms to hand out as gifts

COACHELLA	CONDOR EAGLE SACRED MEDICINE FESTIVAL	ENVISION FESTIVAL	FORM
Empire Polo Club, Indio, California	Alto Paraiso, Brazil	Beachfront jungle in Uvita, Costa Rica	Arcosanti, Arizona, an architectural Utopia built in Arizona's high desert in the 1970s
Mega music festival on vast polo grounds	Monthlong gathering of renowned shamans from the Amazon and beyond leading ceremonies and workshops	Transformational festival dedicated to "awakening our human potential"	A music festival and creative retreat
Sahara tent for late-night EDM dance-a-thons	Ayahuasca	Luna Stage dance floor	Solange, Skrillex, James Blake
Pool parties in Palm Springs	Toad venom	Covering yourself in "healing mud" by the beach with hundreds of others in thong bikinis and loincloths	Organized by the band Hundred Waters, the festival is free but invitation only. If you don't have an invite, fill out an online-submission form. When there, everyone pitches in to help.
Crocheted bikini top loaned by brand in return for an Instagram post, denim microshorts, eight-hundred-dollar round John Lennon–style sunglasses	Loose-fitting white cotton clothes	Heads shaved on the sides and long hair on top, ear piercings, mud between toes	Southwestern ponchos and silver space pants
Procure, by any means necessary, dozens of VIP passes and wristbands to avoid sunburns and dehydration	Hard-core participants only	Bring sustainable, reef-safe sunblock and Dr. Bronner's castile soap	Try to cozy up to the Arcosanti residents and get invited to their trippy architectural homes. Enjoy desert stargazing from a hot tub.

FESTIVALS

	GARBICZ	GLASTONBURY FESTIVAL	OBONJAN
LOCATION	At a lake in the small Polish village of Garbicz	Nine hundred acres on Worthy Farm, Somerset, UK	Obonjan Island, Croatia
TYPE OF FESTIVAL	Eco–music and arts festival with bands and DJs from around the world	Original hippie music festival founded in 1970 by a local farmer. Free milk for all!	Transformation festival that lasts all summer long
STAR ATTRACTION	Outdoor night raves playing wellness-tech	Pyramid Stage for superstar headliners	Held on a private island, so rules are few. DJs and holistic workshops—from "manifesting magic" to group hypnosis.
BOHO CRED	Diving into the lake nude	Praying at sunrise around a stone circle in a meadow at the Sacred Space	Camp out in luxe safari tents
OUTFIT	His: Retro-Hawaiian shirt; hers: '80s neon spandex fanny pack	Wellies, negligee, suede vest, tangled hair	Bikinis
INSIDER TIP	Wander in the forest with a cute new friend	Rent a Mongolian-style yurt in Love Fields. And, yes, you can wear Wellies and a negligee together.	BYOTM (bring your own trail mix)

ONDALINDA	OREGON COUNTRY FAIR	SPIRIT WEAVERS GATHERING	WANDERLUST
Careyes, Mexico, a luxe beach resort on the Pacific Coast	The banks of the Long Tom River in Veneta, Oregon	Illinois Valley of Southern Oregon	All around the world
Music and wellness	Crafts and music fair	Women-only gathering for "sharing earth keeper skills, sacred movement and ceremonial magic"	Rotating yoga festival
Mayan Warrior, Guy Laliberté (Cirque du Soleil founder), and other marquee Burning Man DJs	Wandering around	Hundreds of workshops ranging from a braiding circle to Ayurvedic breast massage	Mass classes with hundreds of yogis outdoors or in a main hall
Take the suspended footbridge to the meditation island	Hang out with "the family," friends and relations of the Grateful Dead and Merry Pranksters	Evening crystal-bowl sound-healing ceremony	Join the laughter yoga class
Bare feet and Hermès sarongs	Lots of billowy purple and rainbow tie-dyes and really long hair	White caftans, chunky turquoise rings, indigo shawls, henna tattoos	Ass-tight leggings and matching crop top made of latest sustainable tech fabric
Spend time in the Copa, an enormous spaceship-shaped sculpture that's perched on a cliff	Bring a flute	Refer to everyone as "sister"	Don't eat beans for breakfast

FESTIVAL DOS AND DON'TS

MAKE NEW FRIENDS and expand your network. The more people you meet, the more likely you are to hear about secret after-parties and collaboration opportunities. And who knows? Maybe you'll make a new friend to travel the world with or fall in love.

DO

Compliment people on their outfits. There are so many imaginative costumes out there; don't be shy about letting someone know you like theirs. It's a great icebreaker.

Come up with a friendly opener as a way of approaching strangers. Like "Have I seen you before?" Or something open-ended, like "How's your journey been?" This implies that even if you haven't met, you want to meet now.

Give a cute gift. Palo santo sticks, rose water, biodegradable glitter, photos you take with a Polaroid camera.

Always bring an extra phone charger in case someone is desperate. You will be friends for life.

Perform random acts of niceness. Give big hugs. But it has to be done in the right way or it might seem creepy. If you have a car, offer people a ride.

Use your best pickup line. "Didn't I see you at ____ festival last month? (The festival should be something cool and insider like Garbicz.)

DON'T

Dump glitter on people. Especially not in their hair. It's very hard to get the glitter off, especially if you're camping in a tent for a week.

Take mystery drugs from strangers. A happy headspace could turn into a dark forest very quickly.

Photograph partially clothed people. Unless you ask first.

Use quasi-spiritual pickup lines. Unless you mean them. (See page 63 for the full list.)

Ask people linear questions like "What part of L.A. do you live in?" or "What kind of work do you do?" You won't be transformed or interesting.

FETISH FIRE SPINNER

At Burning Man, can be found at sunrise spinning fire by the fence

Has her own fire-dancing LLC and troupe. Sells flame-retardant clothes and sock poi at festivals to make extra cash

Instead of conventional perfumes, prefers the aroma of sweat, burned hair, and white gasoline

Claims to have started the trend for retro clowning outfits

Never a moocher; always shows up with an extra bucket of fuel for her fire-spinning friends

Dabbles in fireplay fetishes, like fire flogging and fleshing (designs are made on the body with fuel, then lit and quickly extinguished)

POSTAPOCALYPTIC PREDATOR

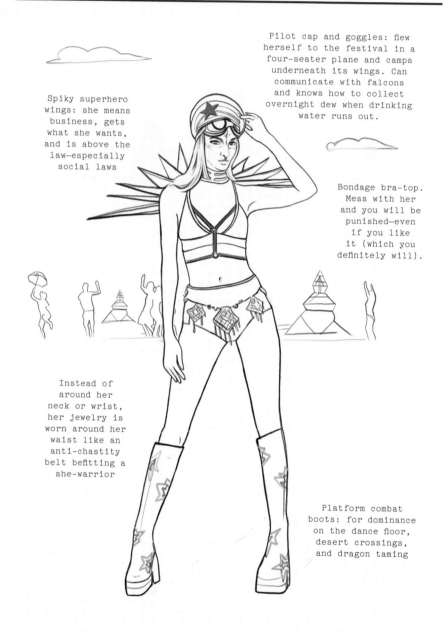

Pilot cap and goggles: flew herself to the festival in a four-seater plane and camps underneath its wings. Can communicate with falcons and knows how to collect overnight dew when drinking water runs out.

Spiky superhero wings: she means business, gets what she wants, and is above the law—especially social laws

Bondage bra-top. Mess with her and you will be punished—even if you like it (which you definitely will).

Instead of around her neck or wrist, her jewelry is worn around her waist like an anti-chastity belt befitting a she-warrior

Platform combat boots: for dominance on the dance floor, desert crossings, and dragon taming

FLOWER CHILD BFFs

Ends of hair dyed in soft rainbow colors for a psychedelic effect

Hippie head scarf makes unwashed hair look cool

Funky felt hat

Flower crown and heart sunglasses in homage to the Summer of Love

Long kimono provides sun protection, warmth at night, and rock star bedroom vibes

Negligee repurposed as daywear. And why not?

Medicine pouch holds a cell phone

Bare feet. Shows commitment to the boho ethos, as they will certainly get stepped on.

Boots to protect toes in case she ends up in the crazy-dancing section by the speakers

BOHO FRONTIER BABE

Can go Wild Wild West all night at an outdoor party but also has a soft domestic side, as evidenced by the floral print duvet and tapestries she brought from home to jazz up her rented tepee.

Could easily lasso horses from the deck of the VIP area

Bandanna denotes fierce independence—she's not afraid to get separated from her friends during the festival

Embossed turquoise vest that she made herself while living in Joshua Tree last spring

Fingers stacked with silver and crystal rings to show off tan and allegiance to the earth's elements

Cowboy boots. Hello, cowgirl in the sand.

BLUE-JEAN BABY

Boyfriend baggy: Shows the confidence that you don't have to look thirsty to be sexy.

Brazilian-cut: Definitely an eye-catcher, but best avoided by anyone over twenty-six—no matter how toned.

Custom club: For the girl who can't resist putting pom-poms everywhere. Eat your heart out, Etsy.

Hippie classic: Very 1960s, when hippie chicks actually cut their jeans when they had too many holes in the knees. Has a DIY sex appeal.

THE SANDAL: HOLY ROAMING EMPIRE

The flat sandal is comfortable and makes no distinction between formal and informal. You can wear sandals to go dancing all night at the beach, climb a pyramid, and dine in an elegant riad.

Here are the staples.

Birkenstocks: These comfortable but ugly shoes were designed in Germany, and, like the VW Beetle, they gained traction in the 1960s after they were adopted by flower children. But despite periodic attempts to make them more conventionally fashionable, like the current candy-colored plastic versions, they require a certain confidence to sport. Good for naturalists and seekers who value purist practicality above all else. (Che Guevara T-shirt not included.)

Espadrilles: The kind with rope soles, please. They should be faded from countless afternoons walking on Mediterranean seaside rocks and exposure to saltwater. They look most boho when worn as a makeshift wedge with the backs pushed down under your heels.

Flip-flops: Go for classic Havaianas, sun-bleached with worn-down soles. Despite the unfortunate urban trend of wearing platform or glittery versions in the aughts, wearing basic flip-flops still shows that you'd rather be surfing.

Greek sandals: Ideally, these are handmade on a Greek island where you shacked up last summer with a guy you met swimming. The sandals should be crafted from earthy, imperfect leather that looks a thousand years old. Be on a first-name basis with the cobbler family at the local market who made them for you.

Gladiator sandals: The gladiator takes a considerable amount of time to buckle up the calf, so it demonstrates either a warrior's commitment to fashion or a kind of OCD kink. Gladiators look particularly fetching when paired with a short Greek-style minidress or microshorts.

Jesus rope sandals: Low-tech and constructed out of twisted rope, the Jesus sandal conveys the message "I care more about spirituality than I do about trends." Less is more, after all. The sandals should look nomadic, like you just walked from Jerusalem to the pyramids and back. Consider hiring a TaskRabbit disciple to wear them for a year first.

CHAPTER 4

GROW YOUR OWN

Philosophical
Farming,
WWOOFers,
and the New
Hyphenated
Cuisine

When Amazon bought Whole Foods in 2017—"Alexa, could you pass the kale?"—it was another example

of a mega-mainstream company going into the healthy food business. Although, Whole Foods wouldn't have been looking for a sugar daddy (organic cane, of course) had its once very profitable health niche not already been colonized—and undersold. In 2014, Walmart partnered with Wild Oats—a former subsidiary of Whole Foods. That same year, General Mills bought Annie's Homegrown, joining once-indie brands like Honest Tea (Coca-Cola owns part of it), Naked Juice (PepsiCo), and Kashi (Kellogg's) in the Big Food roll-up of the natural and organic space.

But boho types—as has been true for those in the anticorporate food revolution—are unwilling to just eat whatever Big Food throws at them through the drive-thru window. Long

before Whole Foods moved into well-educated towns, a network of food co-ops and farmers' markets sprung up, forming a framework that respects both the land and the people who work it. Joining direct-from-the-grower food co-ops, procuring unpasteurized milk, or tending organic gardens (hello, Michelle Obama!) is a political statement as much as a dietary one.

Permaculture, a holistic way of farming, is also a form of activism. Farms around the world, particularly in Central America and Hawaii, are turning into permaculture communities that value natural cycles and the rhythms of the earth as much as they do an organic carrot. Farming, like yoga and tantra, is a form of meditation. And soon you will notice that the earth is breathing just like you.

THE CULT AS RESTAURANT

The Source Family documentary, 2012

IN THE LATE 1960s, the charismatic cult leader Father Yod opened an organic, vegetarian restaurant called the Source on the Sunset Strip in Los Angeles. A prototype for wellness companies, the café was a lifestyle brand before lifestyle brands existed.

Hip-looking cult members with long hair and spacey smiles doubled as waiters, sometimes wearing robes, serving such favorites as the "Aware Salad" and the "Magic Mushroom" (mushrooms, seaweed, and sprouts) to a celebrity clientele that included John Lennon, Warren Beatty, and Julie Christie. The Source was even featured in Woody Allen's classic *Annie Hall* (Allen's character begrudgingly orders alfalfa sprouts and mashed yeast). The cult also had its own psychedelic rock band, Ya Ho

Wha 13, fronted by Father Yod, and the music was often blared at the restaurant. Talk about vertical integration. The little café quickly became the place to be, a trendy emblem of the then-youthful Age of Aquarius. Where you hung out and what you ate was a form of activism. You were choosing an alternative path to a more balanced life—wellness, if you will.

The Source café worked because it not only seemed authentic, it *was* authentic. Yod, a former marine, jujitsu master, and accused murderer, used the proceeds from the café to fund the cult's semi-lavish lifestyle, which included a white Rolls-Royce, a Hollywood Hills mansion, and dozens of pregnant disciples. Influenced by tantra and yoga, his idea was to use the vegan doctrine, along with free love, to show people the light. "Let me be the father you never had," Yod would tell his young followers, who all took on Aquarius as their surname. (See the 2012 documentary *The Source Family* for more info.) Of course, Yod led many of his followers to the opposite of wellness—a reminder that before cultish brands, there were actually cults.

THE RESTAURANT AS CULT

Café Gratitude latte

NOT MANY PEOPLE really want to belong to a cult anymore. Much better to just get your fill of enlightenment and community over a delicious meal.

California-based healthy food brands such as Moon Juice, Sun Life Organics, and Café Gratitude have figured this out. They are all culty without actually being a cult. Walk into a Moon Juice shop in Los Angeles (which looks like a new age laboratory with crystals and wildflowers, and clear-eyed employees dressed in lab white behind the food counter), and witness a dialect made up of terms like "boost," "endocrine," and "cleanse." The name Moon Juice seems very 1970s hippie California era, as do the names of their products, like "Cosmic Cocoa" and "Beauty Dust."

At Café Gratitude, an organic, vegan restaurant chain, every item on the menu is an affirmation. You can order Grateful (a bowl of vegetables and sprouted probiotic brown rice) or Magical (black bean burgers with cashew macadamia cheese). Noshing on anything from the menu is like swallowing propaganda for joy. Mantras of happiness are unavoidable if you want to eat. By the time my Glorious (blackened tempeh Caesar wrap) arrived, delivered by a perky waiter announcing, "You are Glorious," I felt, well, slightly more glorious than before. (Of course, if I weren't open to the culty lexicon, I probably wouldn't be eating at Café Gratitude in the first place.) On the blackboard is a "Question of the Day" that waiters will happily read; it can range from "What do you love about your mother?" (on Mother's Day) to "What are you excited about today?"

Most of the tables are communal, and employees tend to be vegan—it's clear by their yoga-toned bodies and glowy skin that they're believers, too. In fact, one bright-eyed waiter invited me to his didgeridoo recital, a gesture that

overthrew the server-patron barrier in favor of community. I felt like more than just a paying customer—like I belonged to this exotic world somewhat on the edge of my comfort zone.

Using pseudospirituality as branding is tricky terrain, but these healthy food companies navigate it like pros in this social media era. Café Gratitude's cofounder Matthew Engelhart calls it "sacred commerce," a business practice in which his company provides "inspired service, honest and transparent communication, and express gratitude for the richness of our lives."

WWOOFERS

If living on a farm in Maui in a rustic wooden dorm with sweaty, environmentally conscious roommates in denim cutoffs sounds appealing, then you are a good candidate to be a WWOOFer. WWOOF stands for World Wide Opportunities on Organic Farms, and it's a network that connects over 75,000 travelers with live/work farm stays around the world, from New Zealand to Brazil to Italy, specializing in trades such as beekeeping, winemaking, and growing vegetables in the Arctic. Founded in 1971 by a London secretary after she volunteered on an organic farm in Sussex for the weekend with some friends, it has really taken off in the last few years. This generation's Peace Corps, WWOOFing attracts bohos on a shoestring, united over concerns of climate change and unsustainable consumerism. They are fine with postponing careers and a paycheck for the experience of living off the land. WWOOFers work at least four hours per day in exchange for food and shelter and, ideally, a hands-on education in organic farming, although sometimes they might end up mucking out the goats' pen instead of learning how to build a biodegradable straw-bale house. Usually afternoons, evenings, and weekends are free time for waterfall exploration, hikes, and online campaigning against GMOs. Beware of slacker WWOOFers who smoke pot all day and oversleep. Expect hookups, breakups, deep love connections, info trading on cannabis cookie recipes and ride-share apps, and didgeridoo jam sessions under the stars.

Don't bring designer clothing, hair dryers, or monogrammed luggage.

Do bring a pocketknife, a sunhat, and a bandanna.

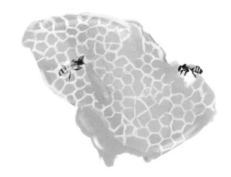

WWOOFER

Joint behind ear;
the marijuana was
grown last fall
during her stint as
a trimmigrant in
Humboldt County, CA

Brown felt hat to keep
sun off in style

Ex-model
turned
environmental
warrior goddess

Bee-stung lips
(actually stung
by a bee)

*The Good Life:
Helen and
Scott Nearing's
Sixty Years of
Self-Sufficient
Living*

Hair beet-dyed
pink at the
ends. All the
girls in the
WWOOFER dorm
did it.

Platter of
just-harvested
fruit for
fruitarian
communal supper

Canteen contains
homemade kombucha
from fermented noni
fruit. Tastes like
baby puke but is
healthy.

In pocket:
iPhone with
apps for
ridesharing
and GMO foods
to avoid

Flip-flops molded to her
feet after being worn
for seven years, the
equivalent of a name tag

Her name is Kale

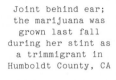

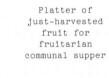

CULTISH FOOD GURU

Coconut oil
dabbed on lips
and eyelids
makes them glowy

Sparkly, clear eyes
from daily green
juice breakfast

Crystal
pendant wards
off health-
shamers

Wooden hot tub filled
with oxygenated,
alkalized water

Carries her
bestselling natural
foods cookbook

Consults her
"vibrational
designer" on major
business decisions

Looks well rested despite
being a mom and running a
business empire

ACTIVIST FARMER

Dreams of moving
to Kauai to join
a community where
they grow jojoba
for biodiesel

Knows that alpacas
are herd animals
and llamas are
more independent

Sweater has bits of
hay stuck in it

Hands are not
that rough—he
freelances as a
graphic designer
in the off-season

Carhartt work
pants

Plays Alice Coltrane
in the background
while milking
cows to calm them
and increase milk
production

Dog's pouch
contains
some endangered
blue corn seeds
from New Mexico

Likes to quote
Michael Pollan's
The Omnivore's Dilemma and
Rudolf Steiner's *Agriculture*

PERMACULTURE CLUB

Permaculture was developed by two Australian ecologists, David Holmgren and Bill Mollison, in 1978 with the publication of their book, *Permaculture One: A Perennial Agriculture for Human Settlements*. It started out as a framework for sustainable agriculture, but soon the system grew to include architecture, design, economics, business, and so on. For Mollison, "permaculture is the philosophy of working with and not against nature, after a long and thoughtful observation." Holmgren described it as "those consciously designed landscapes which simulate or mimic the patterns and relationships observed in natural ecosystems." Heady stuff. You know you're dealing with a permaculture geek if their salad was foraged from a nearby park and they're drinking collected rainwater out of a recycled canteen. I was thinking of having a permaculture dinner party. Diners would get just one plate, a big leaf, and it would be not only reused but also utilized. For example, the juices and sauces left over from the appetizer would complement the main course. Also, you could seat a scientist next to an artist and the artist next to a chef so that even brainpower wasn't wasted.

To be a real permaculture expert, you need to earn a Permaculture Design Certificate by taking a course that entails seventy-two hours of training. Ideally, you would take the course at a pedigreed farm like Bullock's Permaculture Homestead on Orcas Island in Washington State, where students sleep in recycled parachute tents. Upon graduation, you might buy your own farm somewhere, like Colorado, and start an institute subsidized by workshops and renting out camping spots on Glamping Hub (Airbnb for cool, remote camping). And before you know it, someone will stick around longer to help, and someone else will renovate the hayloft into a studio, and soon you'll have your own permaculture community.

PERMACULTURE MUSIC FESTIVALS

What does organic farming have to do with electronic music? A lot, apparently, as permaculture has become the backbone of several music festivals. Envision, an annual music gathering of bikini-clad revelers dancing on the beach in Costa Rica with a crunchy lineup and an emphasis on yoga, is based partly on permaculture, specifically "Regenerative Design, Land Stewardship, Reforestation, Resource Management, Earthcare-PeopleCare-FareShare."

And the Family Gathering, in Taos, New Mexico, founded by a DJ who refers to himself as the Polish Ambassador and wears metallic jumpsuits exclusively, offers DJs, ecstatic dancing, and—wait for it—a three-day permaculture course. The Polish Ambassador calls it "partying with a purpose." He also started the Permaculture Action Tour, in which musicians hit the road with the goal of fusing festival fun with the spreading of permaculture.

"Can impact and celebration coexist in the same environment?" the Polish Ambassador asked on a crowdfunding website. "Can community work parties and projects culminate in ecstatic dance party celebrations? Can we remember that festival culture all began with harvests where people busted their ass for a week(s), all of it culminating in a community celebration known as a festival?"

THE BOHO
KITCHEN

Bohos like food that's scientific and pagan, like their drugs—or shall we say medicine. An added turn-on is if the strange brew or batch boosts the immune system or has anti-inflammatory properties. Here are a few of the staples.

ANYTHING HYPHENATED

Simply having food that's natural, organic, or fresh is not enough. We have outgrown such baseline terms and now demand food whose sophistication requires a hyphen or prefix. Popular terms—with high price tags to match their esteemed health benefits—are "cold-pressed" (a hydraulic press extracts juice from fruit and vegetables, leaving more nutrients), "biodynamic" (farming that's both self-sufficient and in alignment with lunar and astrological cycles), and "probiotic" (foods and potions with good live bacteria). Other trendy hyphenations include—but are certainly not limited to—grass-fed,

free-range, small-batch, heritage-breed, ancient-grain, and gluten-free.

ADAPTOGENS: THE NEW KALE

Instead of offering a glass of wine, you might serve guests a drink made of adaptogens. Adaptogens are an elite class of botanicals—mainly roots and mushrooms with exotic-sounding names like ashwagandha (a root native to India), rhodiola (a plant found in cold regions of the world), and reishi (a mushroom)—thought to improve the body's ability to adapt to stress by lowering cortisol levels in the blood. A staple in ancient Chinese herbal medicine and Indian Ayurveda, adaptogens have overtaken kale as the coolest new thing to pop up on smoothie menus and at the yoga studio café. You can buy them in powder form—or grow them in your kitchen—and make potions by mixing them with almond milk or tea.

Each adaptogen is said to do a slightly different thing, like help clear up skin (tocos), increase sexual energy (cordyceps), enhance memory performance (Panax ginseng), reduce the effects of aging (holy basil tulsi), and boost the immune system (schisandra). Customize the potions as a means of empathy. If one of your friends is feeling down, make her a coconut milk shake with ashwagandha. You can also mix adaptogens with alcohol and make medicinal cocktails and tonics, as some forward-thinking bars have started doing.

FORAGE DU BACKYARD

Requisite and integral to promoting a do-it-yourself ethos, foraging is a way to supplement meals with finds from your flower bed, backyard, or nearby forest such as purslane, lamb's ear, chickweed, and dandelion. Bring a basket borrowed from your parents' house in the suburbs (buying a basket is too bourgeois) to carry the bounty, a sharp knife made by your favorite bespoke maker, and, of course, a field guide to help you identify what's edible and what's poisonous. As you get more familiar with the plants, you can demonstrate your fluency by referring to them as "he" or "she."

MUSHROOM MAGIC

Fungi aren't just for hallucinating anymore. Reishi, chaga, cordyceps, and lion's mane—the big four of functional mushrooms— are said to reduce

stress, support immune functions and cognitive and physical performance, and help maintain gut health.

In Venice Beach, wander down an alleyway off Abbott Kinney Boulevard and find crowds gathered at a tiny kiosk decorated like a forest called Four Sigmatic Shroom Room for cups of mushroom coffee. You can also enroll in their Shroom Academy and become an expert in cultivation and medicinal properties. There are even mushroom gurus like Paul Stamets, a mycologist, author, and advocate. Paul gives talks about mushrooms saving the world at TED and Summit and runs Fungi.com. He believes mushrooms can clean soil and treat virus-caused diseases such as smallpox and the flu. Eat up.

HIGH-VIBE WATER

Water is life and should not be commercialized. Even buying water should be a last resort. Ideally, you get a large glass canteen and hit up a natural spring known for its high-frequency waters, like on Mount Shasta in California. Not sure where the water is? No problem. LiveSpringWater.com will show you where the closest springs are—and even have the water delivered, if you're in range. And if that is out of reach today, try adding crystals to regular water, specifically selenite and amethyst, stones known for their healing properties.

BONE BROTH-ER

Breath smells
like garlic,
cayenne, and
grass-fed butter

Salmon vertebrae
necklace
(for special
occasions)

Cave painting
tattoo

Carton of
wild berries
that he
foraged in
the park

CrossFit
gym bag

Letting his
chest hair grow
after years of
shaving

Starts day with
a cup of frothy
shiitake and
reishi mushrooms
and grass-fed
beef broth

Doesn't wear
underwear

Vibram
FiveFingers
shoes

FERMENTATION GODDESS

Brews her own PMS remedies

Has encyclopedic knowledge of "good" gut bacteria and probiotics

Tattoo of alchemy symbol for fire on her bicep

Sells her natural fragrance made from soil, wild thyme flower, and wood on her e-commerce site. She is also a certified doula.

Fermented chili pineapple is used for microbe-friendly cocktails

Refers to plants as "he" or "she"

Serves kava during parties because she likes the body-melt feel

Wellies

MY MOTHER USED to drag me to health food stores when I was a kid in the 1980s. There was one across the street from our house in Key West, Florida, called, innocuously enough, the Herb Garden. It was dark and dank, with big bins of clumpy grains that reminded me of the wells kids fell into in German fairy tales. The place smelled of BO, patchouli, Bragg Liquid Aminos spray, and nutritional yeast. Sometimes chubby mice sauntered past. Anything that we ate from the Herb Garden, even the tooth-pulling honey granola bars, tasted like live dust. This was true of most health food stores I wandered into during that era. Nobody even thought to apply the word *gourmet*. But not anymore.

Instead of a survivalist storeroom, cutting-edge health food stores have become pristine, white-painted sanctuaries that resemble private museums displaying sacred art. Walking among reclaimed-wood communal tables and bergamot-scented compost bins, one is surrounded by a sea of symbolic words: *natural, earth, sun, moon, whole*.

One need only spend a lunch hour—or "lunch afternoon" as is usually the case—at Erewhon Market in Venice Beach, California, to witness the ascent of this new culture. Launched fifty years ago in Boston as a resource for the then-emerging macrobiotic fad, Erewhon has surfed serial food trends and jumped coasts to secure its current status as the mecca of edible wellness. Wellness—not unrelated to what our parents called "health"—grew up with the food movement, emphasizing the organic, sustainable, nonindustrial, fair-trade-leaning, and holistic.

But whereas food, being a vast, government-regulated (and thus slightly uninteresting) industry, is inherently political as a cause, wellness is more purely personal. It roams free. It has its critics and denigrators—"experts" take regular potshots at wellness mothership Goop, and they may (or may not) be right—but wellness is fundamentally about feeling good and looking like it, too. It has a certain autosuggestive quality: One could sample a dozen of the vegan nut cheeses at Erewhon, and none may taste recognizably delicious, but they all feel extra good.

Erewhon is properly religious in its mission, and appropriately crowdsourced in its product offering. It is a community that self-polices and self-generates. The jammed parking lot can feel like a high noon between those who drive a Prius and those who own a Tesla (with rude interruptions from occasional movie-star Porsches and Ubers waiting for East Coasters recently landed at LAX). Inside, the aisles signal urgency less about lunch than about a particular kind of California yearning: for youth, for perfection, for rebirth. "Ingestible beauty," a more important commodity than groceries at Erewhon, is a uniquely SoCal formulation that whips together various aspects of its boho past: drugs, health and fitness, self-improvement, technological innovation, spiritual exploration. Whenever I'm at Erewhon, I usually run into someone I know who tells me about the curative elixir they're sipping and then invites me to a party, product launch, or kundalini gathering.

The outdoor dining area is perhaps what Laurel Canyon felt like in its full sixties and seventies flow: the epicenter of a new movement and the place to be. Here, the cognoscenti wield yoga mats and network among the shaded picnic tables, sipping a frothy Super Green Potion (with barley grass juice, vanilla stevia, and chlorella). As visitors and voyeurs, we can gawk and judge and wonder why we just spent twenty-five dollars on a jar of the house-made yogurt, but the operative question may be: When is Erewhon coming to our town?

CHAPTER 5

BOHO@HOME

Tree
Houses,
Vacation
Communes,
and Dream
Catchers

The nest is a refuge, and a surefire signal to any visitor that they're not your average normie Tinder catch.

So that means a Balinese daybed instead of a boring Room & Board couch. A yoga mat instead of an exercycle. Instead of a condo, a dome or a tepee. But if you do live in a condo—and hey, most cities are full of condos—be sure to deck it out with macramé and dream catchers and leather poufs from Morocco to give it a "here" but not "stuck here" quality.

For bohemians, design is also about using the homestead as a laboratory for experimentation and change, whether it's their home (and Airbnb funding source),

a group loft, or a weekend commune that's often just a couple hours from the city, where friends can split wood, harvest rutabagas, and get offline.

Or you can just quit your job and find a home far from any rush hour, and perhaps on the Mayan calendar instead. In Central America, communities are popping up where the objective is total self-sufficiency, rules are rewritten, time is told according to the stars, and the party lasts all night.

1. Surfboard won at a contest in Máncora, Peru
2. A set of gamelan gongs for sound baths and/or summoning guests to dinner
3. Leather poufs—duh!
4. Stools instead of chairs
5. '70s Brazilian couch inherited from playboy uncle
6. Chinese art deco rug (also inherited)
7. Moroccan pendant lamps, arranged by a feng shui specialist (who also happens to be the dog walker)
8. Triangular windows in homage to sacred geometry
9. Piles of cushions covered in silk fabric from Thailand purchased after a tantra retreat on Ko Pha-Ngan
10. Macramé wall hanging made by a hippie lady in Ojai
11. Drum as side table
12. Evil eye protector
13. Framed photo of Dad and the Dalai Lama in Dharamsala in the 1990s
14. Guitar, for impromptu jam sessions
15. Indian charpoy daybed, choice spot for ceremonies
16. Uncut crystals mined by hand in Arkansas under a new moon
17. Bolivian frazada throw blanket
18. Stack of books includes *Gypset Style* by Julia Chaplin; *The I Ching Valley of Genius* by Adam Fisher; *The Boho Manifesto* by Julia Chaplin; and *Spaced Out: Radical Environments of the Psychedelic Sixties* by Alastair Gordon
19. Mandala dream catcher

FAVORITE BOHO DESIGN FILMS

A CLASSIC BOHO film doesn't necessarily have to be from the 1960s and '70s—but a lot of them are. Whether it's rock star louche or a secret tropical island, the films listed here all manage to capture the elusive feeling of freedom.

1. *More* (1969), starring Mimsy Farmer and Klaus Grünberg

2. *A Star Is Born* (1976), starring Kris Kristofferson and Barbra Streisand

3. *Performance* (1970), starring Mick Jagger and Anita Pallenberg

4. *I Love You, Alice B. Toklas* (1968), starring Peter Sellers and Leigh Taylor-Young

5. *Barry Lyndon* (1975), starring Ryan O'Neal and Marisa Berenson

6. *The Beach* (2000), starring Leonardo DiCaprio and Tilda Swinton

7. *Easy Rider* (1968), starring Peter Fonda, Dennis Hopper, and Jack Nicholson

8. *The Sandpiper* (1965), starring Elizabeth Taylor and Richard Burton

9. *Wild Wild Country* (2018), starring Rajneesh and Ma Anand Sheela

10. *Zabriskie Point* (1970), starring Mark Frechette and Daria Halprin

HOSTING AND HOUSEGUESTING

Now that you have a beautiful boho home, the guests will come. Boy, will they come! Some will show up for an evening, and some might stay for a month. I met an aristo woman in England who'd discover guests living in certain faraway bedrooms in her castle weeks after the party had ended. How to deal with your guests—and how your guests should deal with you—with or without a castle can be confusing, especially among a group that disdains convention. Here are a few ideas.

THE BOHO PARTY HOST (BPH)

No Emily Post in this house. The BPH encourages misbehavior and absurd breaches of social etiquette. The goal is to create an ambiance of fantasy. To ensure this outcome, try handing out cannabis chocolates or microdoses of LSD to your guests. Let them know they are welcome to disappear at any time to repair to the bedrooms for a disco nap. Encourage sprawling on the floor (on kilim rugs, of course). Give Reiki massages to those with jet lag. Maybe have a flutist dressed like a shepherd performing on the stairs. Most important, the host should make sure that guests don't talk about boring stuff like data plans and traffic. Female BPHs should wear something regal and vaguely psychedelic like a bright-colored

caftan or a turban. Male BPHs should dress elegantly in dark velvets and wear kohl eyeliner.

THE ECCENTRIC HOUSEGUEST (EHG)

The eccentric houseguest (EHG) is someone with an original and compelling backstory and a convincing outfit to inhabit your guest room. It could be a UFO abductee who resides in the Mojave or an artist from Marfa, Texas. EHGs will bring your cocktail parties to life. Their mere presence is enough to lift the quotidian boredom of social obligations.

THE PROFESSIONAL HOUSEGUEST (PHG)

For average nomads, say, from Connecticut or San Diego—not out there enough to be EHGs themselves—don't despair. You can be the person whom those with a cool house want to fill the extra bedrooms with and not be considered a crasher (or a proto–Kato Kaelin).

But how? Charisma and social self-reliance. Never be grumpy from hunger or fatigue. Flirt with your hosts, but avoid polyamorous hookups. Offer to help out with cute chores like picking flowers and curating a brunch playlist, but avoid manual labor. PHGs have an arsenal of self-help parlor tricks to indulge the host. Energy healing, voice lessons, and tarot card readings work well. Anything to get the host talking about their favorite subject: themselves. In the afternoon, collect stones from the beach and make an Easter Island–like sculpture on their deck. Before dinner, offer to forage outside for herbs to put in the salad. (Important: Make sure the herbs are actually edible.) And don't forget to strip your bed upon departure.

QUIRKY COUPLE CAMPED IN YARD (QCCY)

They have 1.2 million followers on #vanlife, but you would never know it. They've been living in their cute VW camper (with makeshift pellet stove and chimney) parked to the left of the garage for over a month and somehow it's never been annoying. In fact, you hardly ever see or hear them except for some melodic wafting guitar at sunset. Despite using your shower infrequently and only when you're at work, they have perfect hippie hair that elicits thousands of likes on their Instagram posts. As does her suede cowboy hat, which she picked up last fall when they were camped out at El Cosmico in Marfa, Texas. He has a degree in ecological engineering from Yale and is always available for stimulating conversation and to fix your HVAC system.

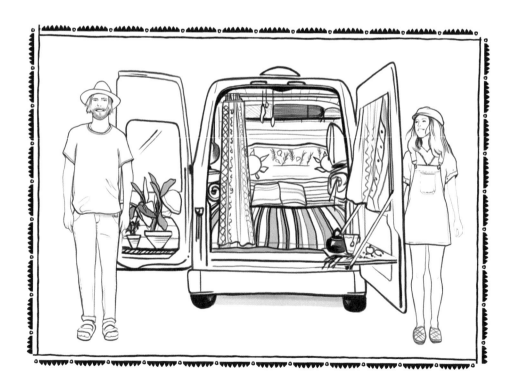

NOMADS DON'T PAY MORTGAGES

Be free, young boho! Live the nomadic dream in a temporary structure set (or parked) in the middle of an old-growth forest, a bucolic meadow, or behind your friend's house. Here are a few options.

Dome: Architect Buckminster Fuller's symbol of progress, found today at Apple and Burning Man.

Tepee: The Native American staple is a favorite of glampers and off-the-gridophiles.

Tree house: The world is more magical when you have to hop a zip line or a rope bridge to get to your front door. Use tree lingo like "treedom" and "tree-shirts."

Van: First choice is a vintage Volkswagen Vanagon or a Winnebago Mercedes-Benz Revel 4x4. #loveit #vanlife

Yurt: No boxed-in feeling here. The hole in the center of the roof represents the connection between earth and heaven.

FOR EVERY DREAM,
A DREAM CATCHER

THE DREAM CATCHER says cool festival goer, vision quester, and possible peyote eater all in one. These funky mystical mobiles are de rigueur in boho homes, perhaps hanging over beds, on side porches, on patios—or likely all three. It is thought that the Native American Ojibwa created the talismans hundreds of years ago to catch bad dreams in the night. They believed spiders were good luck, so the center is made to mimic a spider's web. Bad dreams were caught in the web and the good dreams would slide down the hanging feathers and land blissfully on the sleepers below. Symbolism aside, they look chic, especially when adorned with feathers, bones, shells, and beads. Dream catcher style is a lot like fashion, with statement styles that express personality. Here are some favorites.

Minimal millennial: Wears her mom's vintage jeans, blogs about Ayurveda, shops the farmers' market with a basket she made

Mystical forest nymph: Flamethrows with her friends on the weekends, only wears bamboo panties, sells dream catchers at festivals

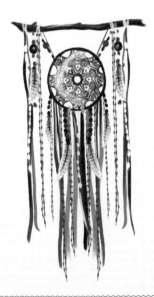

Pink Floyd: Follows Dead & Company, sleeps in tie-dye sheets, smokes a pipe, owns a surfboard that she never uses

Devotee: Does kambo in Grass Valley, spends months at ashrams, is heavily into tarot

Stevie Nicks goth: Home is filled with drip candles and distressed mirrors, only wears black, keeps a whip in the bedroom

CULTURE MASH: HYBRID DECORATING

To set your home apart from all the others on the boho block, you will need to hone a fusion style that mixes cultures and references. You've traveled the world; your home should show your elegant mix of cross-cultural understanding. And no, a fresh-from-the-box faux-shabby-chic Nola rug from Crate & Barrel won't do.

Adult playground: The bohome should incite palpitations of freedom. Playfulness is encouraged with, say, a swing in the living room or a hammock. On the deck, a hot tub—that enduring symbol of free love. And, of course, piles and piles of floor cushions, which provide impromptu sleeping areas for overflow guests and make it much easier to find yourself making out with the sexy shaman's apprentice next to you.

Bali-Thai: First popularized by Buddhist hippie pot-dealer types who traveled in southeast Asia and combined a bling lifestyle with their newfound spirituality.

Now you can see the look in trendy tantricesque nightclubs and party villas in warm-climate hot spots like Miami (the restaurant chain Tao is a good example). The furnishings are a southeast Asian mash-up of Balinese daybeds, statues of Buddhist and Hindu deities, lotus-flower-shaped fountains, lots of loungey teak furniture, and candles.

Boho Balearic: Balearic refers to the Spanish islands of Ibiza, Formentera, Mallorca, and Menorca in the Mediterranean Sea. The boho Balearic sensibility originates from European hippies who summer on Ibiza, mixed with items they pick up during the winter months traveling through Goa, Kathmandu, and other points east. In

Ibiza, you can tell who the OG hippies are by the carpets layered in their fincas from the western Afghanistan province of Herat—part of the hippie migration in the 1970s. Look for hand-carved chakki tables, low and wooden and traditionally used while grinding up grain into flour, which make great coffee tables. The charpoy daybed, also from India, has a simple wooden frame, with the center usually woven in rope. Put one on the patio for stargazing. Boho Balearic also includes a lot of rough-hewn white linens for the hot summers, with an abundance of ceremonial white parties and a steady stream of houseguests.

Moroccan-Mex: A typical spread would mix cotton Moroccan kilim rugs and floor cushions and hammered brass lanterns with earthy hand-loomed textiles from the Yucatán and leather equipale chairs from Guadalajara. The vibe exudes chic global nomad—and is very popular in Tulum.

Native American Oz: A hybrid style of Native American Indian and festival-loving Australians. The look is minimal and sophisticated—not like the cluttered pileups found in such U.S. strongholds as Sedona and Topanga Canyon. A Native

NONBOHO HOUSEHOLD	BOHO HOUSEHOLD
Plasma TV	Window
Wall unit	Books piled on the floor
Microwave	Vitamix juicer
StairMaster	Yoga mat
Nanny cam	Open floor plan
Fluorescent light	Candles
High-tech alarm system	Open door
Infinity pool	Pond
Media room	Meditation room
Housekeeper	Houseguest
Two-car garage	Surfboard rack
Elevator	Ladder
Four-poster canopy bed	Floor cushion
Bearskin rug	Kilim

American arrow wall hanging or a feathered chieftain headdress might be displayed alone on an expanse of white wall, like in an art gallery, to emphasize craftsmanship and beauty. Aztec-print rugs are laid out over a poured-concrete floor, and perhaps an antler chandelier dangles from a lofty ceiling.

INNER EXPRESSION: THE MEDITATION ROOM

Media rooms, "the man cave," and in-home bowling alleys and gyms used to convey a certain enviable status. These days it's the meditation room that has become the ultimate statement in "interior" sophistication. It's not a crass display of wealth but an investment in inner enlightenment, although sometimes it can be both. An ultramodern glass penthouse, perhaps, or a woodsy cabin, or the attic in your parents' house, the meditation room should exude a Zen calm and womb-like comfort. It is a space for the practice of spirituality, clear of plasma TVs and movie posters. You cannot have too many deities, crystals, dream catchers, and rugs. Depending on where you fall on the purist spectrum, your meditation room may also double as a cozy spot for vaping or enjoying tantric trysts. So when possible, make sure upholstery is machine washable. And have the following gear on hand.

Crystals: I met an actress from Byron Bay who spends a good part of the year on the road filming, living in hotels and Airbnbs. In order to stay centered, she travels with a large suitcase filled with crystals (I made the mistake of helping her carry that bag to the car), and when it's a full moon, she takes her collection out to the garden to bathe in the rays and clear its energies. It's good fun to learn the properties assigned to each crystal. For hot dates, try putting carnelian and orange sapphire or rubies in your jeans pocket to ramp up the sacral chakra, which governs sex organs.

Malas: Prayer beads used in Eastern religions to help keep count while repeating a mantra. The beads are made of seeds, wood, bone, or semiprecious stone.

Mandalas: The boho equivalent of a Che Guevara poster hanging in a dorm room, the mandala is a symbol of indoctrination. (*Mandala* means "circle" in Sanskrit, and it represents the infinite universe.)

Palo santo sticks: A groovy South American alternative to sage, palo santo, which means "holy wood" in Spanish, comes from a mystical tree. When sticks of the wood are burned, the "uplifting" aroma keeps energies grounded and clear—and as if that were not enough, it also acts as a repellent to mosquitoes and other pesky bugs that might distract you from meditating.

Socks: Cold feet while meditating are a major bummer (rivaled only by a cramped calf muscle or a wedgie). And while overt fashion statements are frowned upon in meditation settings, socks are a way to sneak in some sartorial sizzle. Try ones with rainbow toes to convey a cute and carefree vibe. A hemp-green pair could signal "environmentalist." Or for the refined sophisticate, go with black cashmere.

1. Chakra painting
2. Feather from a white-winged dove spotted during vision quest in Joshua Tree last year
3. Brocade damaru tail
4. Candles in lotus-flower holders
5. Mardi Gras bead necklaces to symbolize a connection to New Orleans and as a reminder to keep life festive and joyful
6. Framed photo of rescue dog, Mo
7. Incense
8. Crystals
9. Wristband from opening night of Pacha nightclub in 1980
10. Satin wrap for Buddhist text
11. Talismans
12. Wildflowers
13. White mala-bead prayer necklace made of lotus seeds, which represent new beginnings
14. Offering bowl atop pedestal with a few small peyote buttons, a souvenir from time spent with a *peyotero* in the Chihuahua desert
15. Prayer flags
16. Quan Yin, the goddess of compassion
17. Lakshmi, the goddess of wealth, fortune, and prosperity
18. Ganesh, the elephant god of wisdom and learning

DROPPING OUT 2.0

BUILDING A TREE HOUSE
ON SOCIAL MEDIA

Skate ramp at Cinder Cone

FOSTER HUNTINGTON WAS living in New York City, a rising star in the menswear design department at Ralph Lauren, where he helped create aspirational clothing for the faux-outdoorsman. After a year or two, Foster decided to become the aspiration. So he did what barely anyone does: he quit his job, bought a—yes—1987 Volkswagen Vanagon, and meandered around the country. (He wrote a book about the experience: *Home Is Where You Park It.*) In the process, he created the wildly popular #vanlife, which has tags from millions of followers who zealously post photos of themselves and their lovers cooking on scenic bluffs.

But Foster tired of the nomadic #vanlife grind and settled on a parcel of pristine forested land that his parents owned twenty miles west of Portland, Oregon. His plan was to build a dream compound. And that is what he did. Armed with an iPhone camera, he enlisted his good-looking Colby College buddies to don work

Foster Huntington outside the Octagon, the top structure of the Cinder Cone tree house

belts and flannel shirts and build what the *New York Times* dubbed "Brotopia." It slowly evolved, with every sweat bead documented, into a droolworthy homestead with tree houses connected by rope bridges, a sculptural concrete skate bowl, and a wood-fueled outdoor hot tub. Foster named it Cinder Cone, for its setting atop an old volcano. The images of Cinder Cone were beamed around to his followers @fosterhuntington, depicting a preindustrial carefree life of Douglas firs, mountain vistas, power tools, and muscly young men who look like they majored in environmental studies diving off rocks into the Columbia River. Foster has parlayed his nature-man lifestyle into modeling gigs and a self-published book about Cinder Cone. And now he has begun converting the compound into a millennial version of Lucas Ranch with a state-of-the-art film studio for his stop-motion animation films and other experimental projects. Dropping out has never looked so good or paid so well.

SEX, LOVE, AND LICE: A SELECTIVE TIMELINE OF COMMUNES

Experiments are always more fun with a group. And so throughout history, the disillusioned and idealistic, aligned by ideology—free love! no rules!—have gone off into the woods or deserts together to form their own communities and re-create society. Sometimes it works out, and other times it doesn't. It's the effort that counts.

1800S: ONEIDA AND NEW HARMONY

During the Second Great Awakening, utopian communes began popping up around the United States—usually funded by wealthy men who wanted to test out their nutty social ideals. There was the religious Oneida community in New York, founded by John Humphrey Noyes, in which (among other odd rules) every man was married to every woman, although sex and childbirth were heavily regulated. Think a 1940s communist factory, not Haight-Ashbury. New Harmony was a small town in Indiana owned by Robert Owen, a Welsh reformer trying to create a socialist society with equal rights, education for all, and the sharing of property. (But no religion.) He invited everyone to join. But the community failed after a few years when too many freeloaders showed up and Robert Owen almost went bankrupt.

1920S: ABBEY OF THELEMA

Aleister Crowley consulted the I Ching and established the Abbey of Thelema, a commune in Cefalù, Sicily. He and his followers wore robes, performed sun rituals, and practiced the libertine religion he made up, called Thelema.

1965: DROP CITY

Drop City was an architecture commune in southeastern Colorado founded by a group of art students in the mid-1960s. Inspired by the ideas of Buckminster Fuller and Steven Baer, they purchased seven acres of land and invited people to construct their own wacked-out dwellings, mainly domes and geometric

Drop City domes, Trinidad, Colorado, 1967

buildings, made of everything from car roofs to salvaged rubble.

1968–PRESENT: BLACK BEAR

A handful of hippies bought a ghost town in Northern California's Siskiyou County. Their motto? "Free land for free people." Members were forbidden to have sex with the same person for more than two nights in a row (then everyone got VD). The commune is still operating today, with some major changes to the rules.

1969: TAYLOR CAMP

Taylor Camp existed between 1969 and 1977 on seven acres of jungly beachfront on the Hawaiian island of Kauai. The land was owned by Howard Taylor, Elizabeth Taylor's brother. Hippies and draft dodgers lived in makeshift tree houses and shanties and formed a self-sufficient community with a mayor, a sheriff, a food co-op, a public water system, and several churches, including the Church of the Brotherhood of the Paradise Children. Everyone wandered around naked and pregnant. It worked until it didn't. Eventually, drugs, lice, sexual assault, and poverty took over, and the settlement was burned down by the authorities.

1970S: ARCOSANTI

Arcosanti, an architectural community in Arizona, was the brainchild of Italian visionary Paolo Soleri, a student of Frank Lloyd Wright's. It was intended as a futurist city with eco–space age dwellings and a lot of Italian olive trees. Today, Arcosanti, which was only partially built, functions more as an experimental architecture laboratory and supports itself by selling ceramic clay bells and through their Form festival.

1975–PRESENT: DAMANHUR

Falco Tarassaco's laboratory and ecovillage for the future of humankind is in the foothills of the Italian Alps, where four synchronic lines (underground energy rivers) meet. Followers are given names of plants and animals, and practice meditation, magic, and time travel in a series of psychedelic

underground temples inside a mountain. Damanhur is still operating, with about 2,500 people living there. The public can apply for workshops and tours.

1978–PRESENT: TAMERA

This hyperorganized peace research community was founded by a group of German progressives in the 1970s who moved to southwestern Portugal in 1995. The idea is to create "autonomous decentralized models for a post capitalist world." Using permaculture and other farming techniques, they transformed a barren swath of land into fertile grounds with springs and farming that sustain the community of about 250 residents and hundreds of students who come to attend workshops. Popular points of study are the Love School and a political ashram for raising world consciousness.

THE COMMUNE
GOLD COAST:
CENTRAL AMERICA

Cheap land, fertile tropical soil, and more cheap land has made the old-school idea of the communal utopia possible again. Here in the thick jungles and secluded palm-shaded beaches of Central America, thinkers and creatives can buy off-the-grid Edens in which to incubate whims between surf sessions and ceremonies. The region—mostly in Costa Rica but also in parts of Panama and Nicaragua—has become the Gold Coast of communes.

Cofounded by photogenic millennial Jimmy Stice, Kalu Yala is part summer camp, part real estate development and sustainable village on five hundred acres in the Panamanian jungle with solar power and interns (all documented in a reality TV show on Vice). "Let's make some money. Let's live our dreams. Let's share them with the world" is their tagline. You can rent an orange nylon tent for $170 per night, buy a sustainable home, and, if you decide to stick around, even launch a start-up company.

Punta Mona is a well-organized permaculture community on the Atlantic coast of Costa Rica that's suitably remote and accessed only by a muddy trail. They have an extensive organic farm and hold workshops on plant medicine and fermentation. And Pachamama is an ecological and spiritual community in the Guanacaste province of Costa Rica's lush Pacific Coast. These vacation communes, as I call them affectionately, all have aspirational websites featuring tanned communards in yoga poses and quotes about saving the earth and yourself. Visitors are welcome, but they must book rooms in ecolodges and enroll in educational programming or retreats.

Rent is what separates a commune from a vacation commune. At Pachamama, for example, you might sign up for "calligraphy yoga" or a "vision quest"—four days of solitude, prayer, and fasting in the forest. And for those looking to stay a while—a few more weeks or years—there always seems to be an extra room.

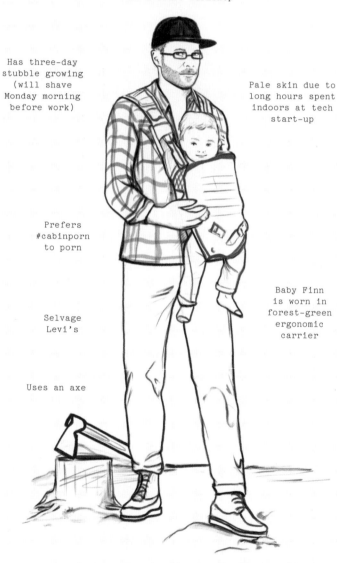

Leather hat that he made
at a craft workshop

Has three-day
stubble growing
(will shave
Monday morning
before work)

Pale skin due to
long hours spent
indoors at tech
start-up

Prefers
#cabinporn
to porn

Selvage
Levi's

Baby Finn
is worn in
forest-green
ergonomic
carrier

Uses an axe

Tousled hair
hasn't been
brushed since
Thursday

Army jacket—a
sample from her
line of modern
maternity clothes

Breton
nautical
striped
shirt
reveals
prep-school
past

Fingers pruned
from too much
time in hot tub

Crocheted bikini bottom
that she made last
weekend, with matching
skullcap (bikini isn't
waterproof)

Short fingernails

Hiking boots

Rescue dog;
half husky

LOFT AS SOCIAL LABORATORY:

THE SAFEHOUSE, SAN FRANCISCO

At Safehouse, a 1972 31-foot Airstream Sovereign Land Yacht serves as a doctor's office

IT'S EASY TO spot Safehouse, an industrial building in San Francisco's Mission District, because it looks like it's wrapped in a lawn. The vertical patchwork of colorful grasses, flowers, and vines is instantly recognizable to ecophiles as a "living wall"—plants and grasses attached to a metal grid structure on the wall, with soil and a watering system that both insulates the building and produces oxygen.

Safehouse, like other experimental homesteads, is a home, a guesthouse, a business, and a social laboratory—the project of entrepreneur Matt Wiggins, a handsome guy who on the day I visit drives up in a dirt-splattered Range Rover with his dog and girlfriend. By way of introduction, Matt leads me inside to a communal kitchen with chalkboards and a long table and makes me a smoothie. Different projects happen in various rooms concurrently. On the ground floor is the former production kitchen of the health restaurant chain Café Gratitude, owned by friends of Matt's who still hold monthly suppers there. At this moment, several young cooks are intently chopping away. They are independent food purveyors without access to a licensed kitchen who rent out the space—a sort of culinary WeWork.

A side door leads to a cavernous area that was once the garage but now has a rainbow-painted planked ceiling and a large Airstream trailer parked inside that Matt rents out when he's not using it as lodging for one of his social experiments. Lately Matt has been populating the loft (the Airstream plus additional bedrooms upstairs) with the aging founders of Burning Man and Esalen Institute as part of a think tank on how to improve elder care. One idea they came up with is to have apartment complexes where the younger residents pay less rent in return for helping the older residents a certain number of hours a week. Matt and his father own a value-based care company, and the idea seems to be gaining traction in the mainstream.

Toward the back of the garage is Matt's office, where he comes up with strategies and workshops them with other entrepreneurs and investors. Up on a mezzanine is a woodworking shop/ recording studio where some artists and makers are working. Matt and his girlfriend keep a bedroom upstairs, but they also have a place to escape to up in Marin County. Various houseguests inhabit the other bedrooms; between sessions on their laptops, they move from a homemade sauna to my favorite zone, a roof tricked out with a hot tub and a big parachute-covered chill-out area with views of the skyline. After the tour—it being Sunday morning in San Francisco—Matt invites me to go with his ex-girlfriend to a tantric sex class. If I want to go, he says, she will swing by and pick me up in forty-five minutes.

CHAPTER 6

MEET THE
NEW BOSS

Hugs, Not Handshakes:
The Rise of the
Boho Entrepreneur

Counterculture capitalism—it's (really!) not about the money.

Work should be just one more path toward enlightenment and personal freedom—not working your ass off at a job you don't believe in only to rack up more credit card debt. Why toil away at a corporation if you don't like its politics—or if the products it sells seem sketchy? The goal is to earn money—but only through a worthy endeavor. Success might mean starting a disruptive company that makes the world a better place, one that VCs (venture capitalists) adore, so you can afford to drive a matte black Tesla and vacation in remote surf spots. But just as impressive, given the required level of commitment, is the entrepreneur who works out of a fifth-floor walk-up studio apartment and cobbles together a relatively meager living as an energy healer and maker of palo santo–scented soap and still manages to vacation in remote surf spots. The point is to make a difference with a socially conscious business of your own—big or small. Bohos aren't snobs about tax brackets, only about how enlightened you are about what you do.

Nobel laureate Professor Muhammad Yunus describes companies designed to solve social problems as flourishing when they shift ideals. Helping out—not getting rich—is the goal. And it is among these conflicting impulses that the boho entrepreneur splashes around. One of Yunus's concepts is that no one should sit around waiting for a job. Cavemen didn't send out résumés, he reasons, and neither should you. Instead, create the job you want—the ultimate in entrepreneurial philosophy. There will be failures, but it's the collective effort and optimism that make this moment so unique.

THE BOHO BUSINESS MEETING

1. Venture capital guy: Made his first million by investing in a coffee chain in Portugal. He's into ayahuasca, lives in Malibu, and drives a Tesla.

2. Social connector/entrepreneur: Organizes community gatherings and has an organic chocolate company she started out of her kitchen. Cuts her own bangs. Fingers still pruned from the morning spent in a float tank.

3. Influencer couple from Australia and high-vibe surfers: Supporting their lifestyle through posts on social media. Her tunic is a prototype made of sustainable Tencel fabric. She needs funding for her start-up.

4. Progressive restaurateur: Runs a locally sourced food business. Spends weekends on his organic farm in Ojai. Arrived to meeting on a vintage motorcycle.

5. Model turned sustainable swimwear designer: Prefers to sit on floor in lotus position.

6. Rolled-up yoga mat for impromptu stretch breaks

7. Attendees raise talking stick when it's their turn to speak

8. Pouf doubles as laptop table

9. Crispy kale chips

10. Pot of rooibos tea

• Meeting starts with a five-minute intention-setting meditation

THE SOCIAL NETWORK

The tech world took the hippie ethos of bartering and commercialized it with sites like Kickstarter, eBay, and Airbnb. Stewart Brand, the famed Stanford-educated biologist/hippie who coined the term "personal computer" and launched the *Whole Earth Catalog* in the 1960s, was a forebearer of "collaboration" society. Brand promoted the egalitarian idea of taking technology used by the military and corporations—as well as other skills that enabled an off-the-grid do-it-yourself lifestyle such as goat husbandry and instructions on building a geodesic "domestead"—and offering it up to the progressive-leaning longhaired masses, something he called "Access to Tools." Even if you weren't planning to have a midwife-assisted water birth, just knowing that you easily could stoked the imagination of a generation.

Brand's attitude is the philosophical backbone of how neobohos do business these days. He was also a Merry Prankster and helped organize the Trips festival held in the mid '60s, which no doubt contributed to the ethos. Hugs over handshakes! Friends want to do business with friends—and with (honest) people who share (nonselfish) values. And so networking on the dance floor is totally fine. Enabled by social media, having a fat network of friends—and friends of friends who can be potentially tapped—all over the world has never been more important. An army of supporters and followers is hard currency.

But in order to have friends, you have to be friendly. "You're beautiful, man!" was a 1960s slogan. But lately I find myself using the word *beautiful* frequently and without irony. I actually mean it. Swaths of neobohos are working toward becoming nicer and more "beautiful" and eradicating bad vibes. When you add beauty to the balance sheet, it fundamentally alters the feeling of a transaction. At least that's what people are hoping will happen. Only time will tell if you can get rich by being "nice" and "beautiful." Of course, that may depend on how you define "rich."

NO MORE 9 TO 5: THE BOHO WORKSCAPE

The corporate ladder is more of a rope swing these days. So set an intention and get with the new mind-set.

COWORKING SPACES: LUNCH HOUR MEDITATION AND MATCHA LATTES

Coworking spaces began to sprout up like mushrooms after a rain when the world economy tanked in 2008. Laid-off workers suddenly stuck at home reinvented themselves as a free-agent workforce. Soon, however, they grew lonely and depressed (still in their pajamas at noon, cereal bowls littering the couch, not talking to other humans for days). Enter the coworking space, and now they are happily waking early to a REM-sensitive alarm and spending the day at places such as WeWork, with over 170 locations around the world from Peru to Australia to Chicago, and NeueHouse, in New York and Los Angeles, where other like-minded aspirants lounge with laptops and matcha lattes on deep leather chill-out couches. It's café society with better lighting and Wi-Fi.

CREATIVE JOB TITLES

It's requisite for boho entrepreneurs to have a cool title for business cards or websites. Something catchy that pays homage to a traditional job title but turns it on its head. Some examples: "tech philosopher," "idea DJ," "epiphany addict" (TV personality Jason Silva), "longevity coach" (Blue Zones' Dan Buettner), "ecopreneur," "spiritual diplomat" (the Polish Ambassador, a DJ and activist), "social alchemist" (Bear Kittay, former Burning Man ambassador), "lifestylist" (Luke Storey, a

The Assemblage NoMad coworking space, New York City

once again allow our species to live, work, and exist on the move. Budapest, Berlin, Bangkok, and Barcelona are the top-rated cities, according to Nomad List; their criteria takes into account air quality, internet speed, walkability, and peace. Another popular hangout is Ubud, Bali, termed "Silicon Rice Paddy" by Tribewanted, a coworking brand. Ironically, these cities are the same ones inhabited by slackers in the 1990s. Are digital nomads and wandering entrepreneurs just slackers with Wi-Fi? Or were slackers simply misunderstood vagrants in a pre-tech era that valued a corporate structure? Probably a little of both.

transformational coach), "pussy priestess" (Josefina Bashout, a love and life coach), "leisure scientist" (that's mine!).

LAPTOPS IN PARADISE: WORKING REMOTELY

Remote working facilities, which often look like a cross between a hip coffee shop and a dentist's waiting room, are popping up in choice vacation spots and low-cost slacker havens around the globe. So there's no need to suffer all year under the fluorescent lights of the thirty-third floor.

The term "digital nomad" is often attributed to a 1997 book, *Digital Nomad*, by Tsugio Makimoto, a Japanese semiconductor scientist, and David Manners, a British journalist. They predicted that technology, combined with our natural urge to travel, would

TIME-SHARE FRIENDS

If you're flitting from one cool city to the next, it's hard to have a steady stream of friends who just show up with a smile to have dinner with you at 9:00 p.m. Global wanderers, despite feeling free, can feel very lonely. So Roam, a coliving and coworking brand, provides friends, or what they term "community." You can touch down in Tokyo, rent a room for a very reasonable eight hundred dollars a week at Roam's "space age '70's"–looking apartment building, and have an instant posse with which to club hop, sample local *izakaya*, or take a sunset stroll.

On a more grassroots level, I met a surfer with a PhD in physics named Garrett Lisi in the surf town of

DIGITAL NOMAD

Three man-buns

Business attire
suitable for any
climate or occasion.
For a night look,
removes the T-shirt.

Travels the world with
just a weekend bag
because in addition to
swapping houses, he
also swaps wardrobes

Smartphone has
screensaver photo
of him with both
girlfriends—he's poly

Neon rainbow
wristband
from recent
CryptoPsychedelic
Summit in Tulum

In bag, carries
headphones (to drown
out noise in coworking
cafés), personalized
stationery for
handwritten thank-you
notes, and a prototype
of a new MacBook that
he's consulting on

Wears flip-flops
as work shoes

LIFE-HACK PHILOSOPHER

Doesn't really need glasses but likes the nerd look

Prefers flesh-colored headset but they were all out

Carries *The Truth Machine: The Blockchain and the Future of Everything* by Paul Vigna

Statement necklace made of beads and antler

Rope friendship bracelet given to her by BFF Gwyneth Paltrow

Tote bag is from Singularity University, where she gives frequent lectures

Technical fabric dress pants keep their shape from the plane to the stage

Her lecture on the power of empathy in the workplace was the most viewed on TED last year

Paia, Maui. When I visited, he had a construction crew hammering away at his verdant hillside property, erecting several wooden cottages intended for scientists who wanted to come to Maui and work on theorems and surf for a few weeks or months. Garrett wanted other boho scientist types to build guest cottages on their properties and allow him to skip across the globe using this grid of free lodging. Down with resort taxes and tables for one.

LIFE HACKS

How do you turn vacations into a mini retirement? Or answer all your emails without reading any? Being a successful entrepreneur requires life hacks—simple tricks to make your life more efficient.

The 4-Hour Workweek by Timothy Ferriss is the neoboho bible, filled with useful tidbits to "escape 9–5, live anywhere, and join the new rich." Ferriss calls it "lifestyle design." He has life hacks for time management, unplugging, and outsourcing jobs. There's advice including "The Low Information Diet: Cultivating Selective Ignorance." (For one week, "No newspapers, magazines, audio books, or nonmusical radio. Music is permitted at all times." Then fill the freed-up time with "speaking to your spouse and bonding with your children.") Another goodie is "Disappearing Act: How to Escape the Office." ("Suggest only one or two days in the office per week.

Make those days the least productive of the week. Suggest complete mobility—the boss will go for it.")

You likely will not agree with all of one guru's life hacks. In the chapter "How to Travel the World with 10 Pounds or Less," Ferriss recommends stuff like a pair of Reef sandals and two pairs of ExOfficio lightweight underwear. Personally, I like Havaianas flip-flops, a one-piece bathing suit that doubles as dinner attire, and a sarong that can be a blanket, a dress, and a towel. So don't follow blindly but mix and match life hacks and come up with a plan that makes you successful without having to work that much.

Tribewanted Monestevole, Perugia, Italy

THE ETERNAL TEENAGER

Nothing is a more beneficial waste of time than board sports, including surfing, snowboarding, kiteboarding, and skateboarding. These activities can swallow up hours or years of your life, causing you to miss work when the surf is up or the powder is falling. Not to mention that you will need to travel to far-afield places to access the best conditions. It's practically a full-time job tracking storm swells and waiting out winds and tides—teenagers can do it so much more easily than workaday adults—but the feeling of unbridled freedom and raw adrenaline coursing through your veins will keep you young.

Which is why these so-called dropout sports are so appealing to bohos. They symbolize a new set of priorities—health and happiness first, work later! Feel alive! Cool companies such as Patagonia recognize this. Patagonia founder Yvon Chouinard wrote a how-to-succeed-in-business book called *Let My People Go Surfing* about allowing his employees to skip work whenever the waves were "six feet, hot, and glassy" as a means of keeping them productive and sane. Back in the '50s, surfing was the sport of dropouts and beach bums, but now board sports are regarded as the wellness tonic they really are. Not to mention an excellent networking opportunity. Bonding over surf breaks and backwoods snowboard trails is the boho equivalent of trading stock tips on the golf course.

HOW TO MAKE UNEMPLOYMENT SEEM COOL

It's always so refreshing to hear someone answer the annoyingly linear question "What do you do?" with "Um, well, I'm in transition right now." While unemployment used to be regarded as a contagious plague and the admission of it made strangers bolt for the bar, now it's a completely charming and acceptable response. Delivered in an optimistic and mysterious way, it exudes an entrepreneurial confidence. You are not just a cog in the wheel, after all; you are "taking time" to "evaluate and weigh" your "options." Your next big thing. It implies that you've already done something big (and if that's not true, definitely don't say anything). Upon hearing the mellifluous term "transition" roll off your tongue, people will try to help you. They may attempt to recruit you for their own projects (in your malleable state, you are prime follower fodder for a microguru), or they may confide in you about their own dissatisfaction. Regardless, unemployment has never carried so much cachet.

FREE SURFER

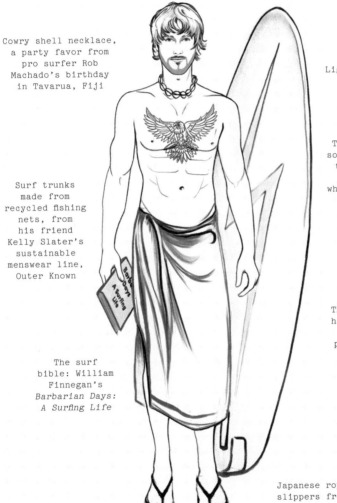

Bowl haircut
actually cut
with a bowl

Cowry shell necklace,
a party favor from
pro surfer Rob
Machado's birthday
in Tavarua, Fiji

Lightning Bolt
surfboard

Tattoo of a
soaring eagle
to express
feelings
while getting
barreled

Surf trunks
made from
recycled fishing
nets, from
his friend
Kelly Slater's
sustainable
menswear line,
Outer Known

Throws shaka
hand signals
in the
parking lot

The surf
bible: William
Finnegan's
*Barbarian Days:
A Surfing Life*

Japanese rope
slippers from
Kamakura, Japan

SMALL-BATCH FASHIONISTAS

Has a line of
handmade hats.
This one was made
of sustainably
harvested beaver
fur felt.

Traded a hat for
this cashmere
sweater marinated
in saltwater

Uses his family
as hat models

Old Spice
deodorant (worn
ironically)

Wears a wedding
band even
though he's not
married. Not to
ward off women
but to attract a
certain kind.

Uses part-
time modeling
cash to pay for
college, where
he's studying
environmental
sciences and
sustainable
development

Friends
with Diplo

Former pro surfer who
makes eco-wet suits
and yoga mats from
recycled neoprene

Trades bars of
palo santo surf
wax for yerba
mate shakes and
kundalini classes

Hands-free-
uses computer
only on Mondays
and Wednesdays

Only wears clothes
given to her by
friends or that are
vintage. Patches on
jeans sewn on by the
beautiful women in
her goddess circle.

Hosts anti-plastic
rallies and beach
cleanups

Her surf and wellness
retreats are all
wait-listed

Hauls a collection
of crystal bowls for
giving sound bath
meditations

IPO GUY

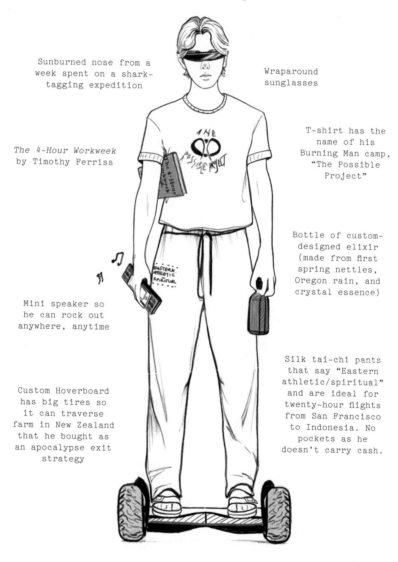

Last haircut was when he was on the grid six months ago

Sunburned nose from a week spent on a shark-tagging expedition

Wraparound sunglasses

The 4-Hour Workweek by Timothy Ferriss

T-shirt has the name of his Burning Man camp, "The Possible Project"

Bottle of custom-designed elixir (made from first spring nettles, Oregon rain, and crystal essence)

Mini speaker so he can rock out anywhere, anytime

Custom Hoverboard has big tires so it can traverse farm in New Zealand that he bought as an apocalypse exit strategy

Silk tai-chi pants that say "Eastern athletic/spiritual" and are ideal for twenty-hour flights from San Francisco to Indonesia. No pockets as he doesn't carry cash.

White Birkenstocks

TOP BOHO
BUSINESS IDEAS

NOTHING IS OFF-LIMITS in the marketplace as long as it's fresh. Worry about profitability later. The ideas should be scalable so that you don't need your parents or an IPO friend as an investor to get started. You can bankroll your venture on Kickstarter. Ask your old graphic designer roommate to come up with a logo in exchange for free product or services.

Celestial event travel agency: Total solar eclipse, equinoxes, comets, and meteor showers (Perseids, Orionids, et al) observed from the world's most advantageous perches, including Mount Fuji, Mount Shasta, and the Sahara Desert. Lodging, rituals, and organic meals included.

Peruvian poncho and lifestyle brand: With a mission to save indigenous peoples, sacred ayahuasca grounds, and the rainforest. Also hosts an annual transformational festival held in the hills outside of Taos, New Mexico.

Nonprofit start-up that helps nonprofit start-ups.

Boho House–type membership club: Gathers in gypset outposts like Tulum, Mykonos, and Venice Beach. Offerings include talks on "Crypto Consciousness" and "Energetic Love and Connection."

Mezcal brand: Artisanal, made by a matriarchal family in Oaxaca, Mexico.

Mars colonization program: À la Elon Musk or Jeff Bezos.

Yoga mats made from something recycled, like flip-flops or obsolete charger cords.

Kombucha home fermentation kits made from the salvaged wood of old Japanese teahouses.

Energetic dating app: Instead of the usual photos and mundane info about hobbies and jobs, this app is based on energetic vibrations. The technology for measuring these is still in development.

THE MILLION DOLLAR(S) IDEA

BLUE ZONES

WANT TO BECOME a self-help guru? First, you will need a catchy idea. A good example is Blue Zones, the brainchild of longevity coach and explorer Dan Buettner, an adventure writer and transcontinental cyclist who holds three Guinness world records.

Here's the concept: Blue Zones are places around the world where inhabitants live longer and are healthier than people in other areas. Those places include the Greek island of Ikaria; Sardinia, Italy; Okinawa, Japan; the Nicoya Peninsula in Costa Rica; and Loma Linda, California, where Seventh-day Adventists have a tendency to outlive their fellow Americans thanks to a mostly vegetarian diet that is heavy on nuts, beans, oatmeal, 100 percent whole-grain bread, and avocados. When Buettner compared these Blue Zone communities, he found nine common habits and values that people everywhere should try to emulate:

• Loma Linda, CA

Sardinia, Italy

Nicoya Peninsula, Costa Rica

1. Natural daily movement—not gonzo gym workouts but biking or walking to work, climbing stairs, and using fewer labor-saving devices

2. A strong sense of purpose in life

3. A plant-based diet with lots of beans

4. Eating less—not fad dieting but smaller portions of nutritious foods

5. Drinking moderate amounts of red wine

6. Making time for ourselves—creating, socializing, napping—in order to decrease stress

7. Attending faith-based services at least four times a month (could be a meditation class or Buddhist lectures)

8. Putting family first

9. Having a healthy social network to talk to and depend on

Buettner puts forth his concept in his three books—all *New York Times* bestsellers—and is a fixture on the ideas festival circuit. His TED talk, "How to Live to Be 100+," has been viewed over 1 million times.

Blue Zones has all the criteria of a successful self-help idea: It references exotic islands in Greece, the promise of happiness and health, and an attainable formula, and the concept is promoted by an inspirational, sexy person with an energetic stare who can sit in lotus position in formal clothing. But the bottom line is, he figured out something people not only wanted but needed to hear, and made the world healthier and happier in the process.

Ikaria, Greece

Okinawa, Japan

IDEAS FESTIVALS: DEEP THOUGHTS AND DANCING

TED talks were launched in 1984 to bring together forward-thinking leaders from the technology, entertainment, and design sectors. Speakers included Bill Clinton, Bill Gates, Google founders Larry Page and Sergey Brin, and hundreds of other innovators whose talks are viral video fodder on YouTube and Vimeo, as in "You should check out so-and-so's TED talk."

Since then, an interesting thing has happened. Nerdy conferences, with back-to-back lectures and name-tag networking in sterile hotel convention halls, have merged with freewheeling, hard-partying festival culture to create the ideas festival. Ideas festivals have lectures and talks but also wellness offerings, progressive cuisine, and lots and lots of parties. And people really, really want to attend these gatherings. They are the new vacations. More fulfilling than vegging on a sun chair by the pool, ideas festivals are regarded as self-enrichment, sort of like getting a rejuvenating brain massage. Sure, you might be making new business contacts, but you're also making new friends who might invite you to their tantric compound in Ojai or to check out a sustainable-housing concept in Kauai. Networking is the goal. Get your start-up funded. Meet your next girlfriend. These things happen, and there's a chance they could happen for you—once you're on the circuit.

Ideas festivals vary in scale and theme. Hatch is held on a ranch in Big Sky, Montana, for a few hundred, and Summit hosts a big, highly produced event in downtown Los Angeles for several thousand. But the through line is progressive speakers ranging from Amazon founder Jeff Bezos to Wim Hof (aka "the Iceman," a daredevil who developed a breathing technique to help people withstand extreme cold). The talks are interspersed with infrared spas, yoga, and sound baths, and there are promotional freebies such as reishi mushroom lattes. The social offerings are big draws—usually some combination

of DJ parties and musical performances with opportunities to duck out at 3:00 a.m. for a Daoist tea ceremony and Reiki massage.

It's easy to get hooked on ideas festivals. There's a certain adrenaline that comes from the tag-team hyperactive socializing—you can make new best friends in the buffet line or on the shuttle bus. It's like the real world, only better and faster.

SUMMIT

YURTS, SNOWBOARDS, AND NETWORKING IN THE HOT TUB

Sunken yurt in the Skylodge atop Powder Mountain at Summit

"WE BELIEVE THE most powerful community-building technologies are the dinner table and campfire." This pitch comes from Summit, an ideas community that operates from atop their own ski resort, called Powder Mountain, in the fittingly named Eden, Utah, with money raised via Kickstarter and some deep-pocketed friends. The founders, four college pals who started out running a business commune in Malibu (they charged money for dinners, salons, events in their live/work villa), are now in the midst of building a village on Powder Mountain. With farm-to-table cafés, coworking spaces, progressive architecture, and ecohotels, it will be a sort of "cool town USA" dedicated to "generational ideals" where the intelligentsia gather to network, snowboard, and party, according to cofounder Jeff Rosenthal. (Summit also holds conferences in downtown Los Angeles and, until recently, on chartered cruise ships.)

So far, the leisure utopia fusion seems to be working. Early residents of Powder Mountain include Toms Shoes founder Blake Mycoskie, *The 4-Hour Workweek* author Tim Ferriss, and Silicon Valley CEOs. (Homeowners must use approved architects, and absolutely no McMansions are allowed!) When I visited for one of Summit's long weekend "jams," I hung out on top of the mountain in an insulated yurt adorned with couches, Aztec-print throw blankets, and a large gong.

Between ski runs, I met with a cross section of amiable neo-entrepreneurs, including a Brooklyn-based dentist who was launching a hemp-derived CBD-oil toothpaste that he said would work wonders on gingivitis; the head engineer for Karma, the electric vehicle company; and a finance guy working for a banking start-up that enables low-income people to accrue wealth by saving and investing a few dollars a week. Lunch was a buffet of organic vegetables and free-range meats that we ate while huddled in the yurt listening to an NPR correspondent interview a former white supremacist who had started a foundation against hate. (Such heady "content" seems to be a way to offset mindless leisure. Shall we coin it "mindful leisure"?)

The crowd ranged in age from sixteen to sixty, but mainly they were good-looking, contact-wielding millennials with the latest high-performance, brand-ambassador ski gear. Almost everyone lived in such liberal cities as Los Angeles, San Francisco, New York, and Austin. The group of about 150 were outgoing; flashing big smiles, making eye contact, and offering chocolate edibles as well as invitations to various condo after-parties—the sort of inclusive, velvet-rope-eschewing friendliness found at Burning Man. It was fun, and I made tons of new best friends, although the edibles were so potent that I forgot to get anyone's contact info, a major networking faux pas. Regardless, as I was driven to the airport at the end of the long weekend by my condo-mate, a coder from Transylvania, in his rented Tesla, I had the hopeful feeling that I was part of an exciting new movement.

IDEAS FESTIVALS

	C2	DO WALES	HATCH
LOCATION	Montreal	Farm in Cardigan, Wales	Big Sky, Montana and Provence, France
ATTENDEES	Entrepreneurs with a twist	Progressive doers	Progressives trying to "reverse the creativity crisis"
TAGLINE	"Transform the way you do business."	"Don't just stand there. Do something."	"Bring together diverse perspectives to HATCH a better world."
WHEN AND DURATION	May for three days	Late June/early July for three days	October, in Montana for four days, and June, in France for four days
LECTURE TOPICS AND SPEAKERS	Chad Dickerson, former CEO of Etsy turned CEO coach; Suroosh Alvi, cofounder of Vice; Martha Stewart	Anna Young, cofounder of Pop Up Labs, a company that runs MakerNurse, a community of inventive nurses looking to improve care, and Jim Brunberg, founder of the Roam Schooled podcast	Haskell Wexler, the late film producer and director; Judy Turner, consultant for Nike, Apple, and IDEO; Nolan Bushnell, founder of Atari
FOOTWEAR	His: English loafers; hers: Céline flats	Wellies	Isabel Marant moccasins
NOTES	A lot of the people here seem to work for Cirque du Soleil	Talks take place in a cowshed. Workshops are held year-round	Make sure to have an idea to pitch

SLUSH	SUMMIT	TED CONFERENCE	WISDOM 2.0
Helsinki, Finland	Powder Mountain, Utah, and downtown Los Angeles, California	Vancouver	San Francisco
iGen techies connecting with investors and executives	Socially conscious millennials	Mainstream movers and shakers	Techies seeking soul
"Where 20,000 tech heads come for more than inspiration."	"Experiences that connect, educate and inspire today's brightest leaders."	"Ideas worth spreading."	"How do we live with greater mindfulness, wisdom, and compassion in the digital age?"
December for two days	Throughout the year on Powder Mountain; a long weekend in November in Los Angeles	April for five days	February or March for three days
Julia Hartz, cofounder and CEO of Eventbrite; Casey Winters, growth advisor; Preethi Kasireddy, founder and CEO of TruStory	#metoo creator Tarana Burke, Diplo, Amazon CEO Jeff Bezos	Bill Clinton, Bill Gates, Google founders Sergey Brin and Larry Page	Jon Kabat-Zinn, founder of Mindfulness-Based Stress Reduction, in conversation with author and scholar Stephen Mitchell
Short Wellies that look good with skinny jeans tucked in	Yeezy sneakers	His: polished; hers: Tod's	Nike Air sneakers
Students help organize the festival, so parties, held in saunas and old factories, are over the top	Don't get too high and forget to network	Best networking is in the greenroom	If you don't meditate, don't tell anyone

EVERYTHING IS MICRO NOW

Micro, micro, micro! Microgreens might come from microfarming (growing everything you need on 2.5 acres) and be accompanied by microbrews (small-batch, high-quality beer), which you know about thanks to data-driven microtargeting (only the right people receive the message). And in the end, what we're talking about is microliving: forget exurban sprawl with guzzler McMansions. Live instead with edited sophistication and style. Big is wasteful, tastes bad, or gets you too high. We are firmly in a micro moment.

ARE YOU A MICROGURU?

I created the term "microguru" to describe the growing, egalitarian ranks of leaders, healers, and teachers. It's like an influencer, but with a higher purpose beyond instilling FOMO or getting you to click on whatever has #sponsored her post.

In the '60s, the Beatles and other seekers had to trek all the way to an ashram in India for an audience with their guru. Gurus were few, and wisdom, for the most part, was consolidated among the robed and bearded. Now that self-discovery, learning, and mindfulness are widespread, guruism is more attainable (like tech gurus or surf gurus). We are in a collective mood to "like" and "follow," as evidenced by social media and the proliferation of retreats and workshops.

And to fill the demand or perhaps create it, an increasing number of people have homed in on a personal message that's easy to spread thanks to sites like YouTube and Instagram and ideas festivals (see page 176).

To be a microguru, you don't need to have gone to India or have any particular training. You simply need minimal to moderate charisma (which can be developed over time; don't worry), a clear message, and a boutique, niche following. And who doesn't moonlight as a Reiki healer these days? The point is, we all have something to teach, and people are increasingly receptive as long as it doesn't take too much time and it makes them feel better than before.

I DECIDED TO become a microguru after I realized that I already was one. Let me explain. I coined the term "gypset" (gypsy + jet set), and while I was writing my books *Gypset Style, Gypset Travel,* and *Gypset Living,* friends, acquaintances, and strangers would email me for recommendations and advice on everything from what hotel to stay at in Bali to whether they should quit their jobs. At parties, strangers would offer me compliments for having come up with an inspiring lifestyle. "You've really figured it out," they'd say. When this first started happening, I would think about all the problems in my life (perennially dwindling bank account, revolving door of boyfriends, etc.) and tell them that despite appearances, I had not "figured it out" at all. I was as confused and lost as everyone else. They always seemed so disappointed with my answer. I began trying to reconcile my image with how I was actually feeling and to think of things differently.

I started focusing on what I *had* figured out—like how to travel frequently and have friends all over the world, a beautiful daughter, and a career I was passionate about. Now when I receive compliments, I say thank you and smile.

When I started thinking about the idea of writing *The Boho Manifesto,* I immersed myself in self-help books, ideas festivals, and any relevant talk or class I could find, from an organic farming seminar to bio hacks for the home. I began to understand that like many of these speakers, I actually had distilled a life-hack philosophy of my own. I had been refining these ideas for years to help myself navigate the world. Now I offer them to you.

MICROWISDOM

- There are no rules. Stop doing what's appropriate or socially expected. Instead, do what you want to, and do it your way.

- Be the sun, not a planet. Find your center, and don't orbit around other people's dreams.

- Embrace randomness and spontaneity. Clear a space in your life for these things to occur frequently. Do go to the weird-sounding art exhibit forty-five minutes away. Experiences are never a waste of time.

- Practice conceptual absurdity. Take silliness much further—that's where creativity lies.

- Meandering and having goals are not at odds. Set goals, but then take a winding, indirect path to get there. It will be much more fun, and you will be more interesting.

Remember, the operative term here is "micro": we are all specks of dust (or grains of glitter) in the macro cosmic sprawl, and the communities we make within it come alive when they're the considered, soul-searched expressions of our explored self. Microwisdom only becomes macro when we choose to share it by fully living. And we only live twice.

ACKNOWLEDGMENTS

Many, many thanks to the generous group of people who provided me with inspiration, knowledge, and perspective on the many facets of the bohemian realm: Andrey Ayrapetov, Blair Edwards, Jesse Hernreich, Katia Tallarico, Kassia Meador, Luke Storey, Carmel Snow, Karla Gutierrez, Laura Fratta, Zach Wolf, Bibi Brzozka, Biet Simkin, Michael Goodwin, Kari Jansen, Tara McManus, Matt Wiggins, Jeff Rosenthal and the Summit family, Nick Kislinger, Dan Harris, the Insight Meditation Society, Claus Sendlinger, Mia, François, Zem Joaquin, Giancarlo and Stephanie Canavesio, Erik Davis, Adam Fisher, Mark Epstein, Stephanie Paine, Brooke Waterhouse, Elien Becque, Meghan Boody, Charlie Gepp, Carl Swanson, Joe Caccamo, Barnaby and Sophie Ferrero, Tanya Selvaratnam, Ipek Irgit, Yves Béhar, Sabrina Buell, Deb Schoeneman, and Leo and Yvonne Force Villareal.

To my family: Diana, Rosie, Avery, Laura, and Susie Chaplin. Eli Sternberg, and Sarah Teale. Jason Miller for ground support. To my parents, Holly Chaplin and Gordon Chaplin, who have always encouraged me to go my own way. And to my daughter, Tuesday Miller, to whom I dedicate this book and who makes every grand adventure even grander.

Thanks to the team at Artisan for the hard work, dedication, and patience, especially Lia Ronnen, Shoshana Gutmajer, Michelle Ishay-Cohen, Sibylle Kazeroid, Nina Simoneaux, Zach Greenwald, Nancy Murray, Hanh Le, and Elise Ramsbottom.

And to Spiros Halaris for his illustrations and diagrams that help bring this world to life.

And to my superagent, Meg Thompson, who always knows what to do.

Special thanks to Carlito Dalceggio for sprinkling joy over these pages with his inspired artwork, which I think perfectly embodies this new bohemian movement; to Vanessa Grigoriadis and Sarita Woody for the valuable insight and taking on the responsibility of being my trusted readers; and James Truman, whose support and beautiful thinking helped the book bloom into something I'm very proud of.

Let the bohemian revolution begin!

xx Julia xx

INDEX

PHOTOGRAPHY CREDITS

JULIA CHAPLIN is a journalist, author, designer, and consultant. She's written and produced three books—*Gypset Style*, *Gypset Travel*, and *Gypset Living*—and is a frequent contributor to the *New York Times*, *Travel & Leisure*, *Condé Nast Traveler*, and *Elle* as well as a founder of the travel company Gypset Collective. When she's not traveling around the globe, she lives in Brooklyn, New York. Find her on Instagram @gypset_official and at gypset.com.

Library of Congress Cataloging-in-Publication Data

Names: Chaplin, Julia, author.
Title: The boho manifesto / Julia Chaplin.
Description: New York : Artisan, a division of Workman Publishing Co., Inc. [2018] | Includes an index.
Identifiers: LCCN 2018003595 | ISBN 9781579657895 (hardcover : alk. paper)
Subjects: LCSH: Bohemianism—United States—Humor. | Alternative lifestyles—United States—Humor.
Classification: LCC HQ2044.U6 C56 2018 | DDC 306/.1—dc23
LC record available at https://lccn.loc.gov/2018003595

Design by Nina Simoneaux

Artisan books are available at special discounts when purchased in bulk for premiums and sales promotions as well as for fund-raising or educational use. Special editions or book excerpts also can be created to specification. For details, contact the Special Sales Director at the address below, or send an email to specialmarkets@workman.com.

For speaking engagements, contact speakersbureau@workman.com.

Published by Artisan
A division of Workman Publishing Co., Inc.
225 Varick Street
New York, NY 10014-4381
artisanbooks.com

Artisan is a registered trademark of Workman Publishing Co., Inc.

Published simultaneously in Canada by Thomas Allen & Son, Limited

Printed in the United States of America

First printing, May 2019

10 9 8 7 6 5 4 3 2 1